*The Rate and Pattern of Industrial Growth
in Communist China*

The Rate and Pattern
of
Industrial Growth
in
Communist China

—

Kang Chao

Ann Arbor
The University of Michigan Press
⊏1965⊐

Preface

Originally, this monograph was prepared in 1962. Although several parts have been revised since then, the framework and computational methods remain unchanged. I regret that I have not been able to extend my indexes beyond 1959 because from 1960 the Communist regime in Peking has tried—quite successfully—to blackout all economic information, especially quantitative data with a nation-wide coverage.

In carrying out this study, I received financial support from the National Science Foundation and the Center for Chinese Studies, The University of Michigan. I herein express my sincere gratitude to these institutes. Funds for the publication of this book were granted by the Horace H. Rackham School of Graduate Studies of The University of Michigan.

Among the persons who have helped me to accomplish this study, my deepest gratitude goes to Professor Alexander Eckstein, who is almost a co-author. Not only was his the inspiration which first led me to investigate this subject, but also he solicited both funds and information on my behalf. Although this book is virtually a joint product, I alone am responsible for any defects which may remain despite Professor Eckstein's countless valuable remarks and comments given in numerous discussions.

I wish to thank Professors Ta-chung Liu, Morris Bornstein, Eva L. Mueller, and Norman M. Kaplan for their valuable suggestions and helpful comments. I am also grateful to the librarians in the Chinese Section of the Division of Orientalia in the Library of Congress and in the Hoover Library at Stanford University, whose special arrangements during my visits enabled me to collect in very short periods of time a great deal of valuable material I could not obtain elsewhere. Special mention should be made of the price handbook of industrial materials and equipment in Communist China, which I discovered, during my short visit to Stanford in February 1961, in the wonderful collection of Chinese Communist publications in the Hoover Library. To the best of my knowledge, this was, and still is, the only price handbook of a general nature available to academic scholars on Communist China in this country. Without it I could hardly have solved the intra-industry weighting problem in my study.

Contents

CHAPTER I

Introduction

Ever since the outset of Communist China great emphasis has been placed on developing industry in the hope of converting a backward agricultural country into an industrial nation on a socialist basis. This extensive drive for industrialization is evidenced by the large share of the total investment funds that was devoted to industry in each year during the First and Second Five Year Plans. Table 1 indicates for each year in the period from 1952 to 1959 the amount of so-called "basic construction investment" in industry, which is the Communist term for investment of fixed capital going into the industrial sector, and its proportion to that for the whole economy.[1]

To assess the success of China's industrialization program and the actual growth of industrial output, a reliable measure of industrial production is needed. Yet, it is widely recognized by Western economists[2] that Communist China's official output index contains upward biases which make it very unreliable for this purpose.

The present study attempts to bridge this gap by constructing an independent index of the industrial output produced by Communist China in the period from 1949 to 1959 primarily based on the officially published data of physical output. We could not extend the index to years after 1959 because almost no physical output data have been divulged since then.

1952 is chosen as the base year because it was the demarcation point of the economic development in Communist China. Up to 1952 was primarily the phase of recovery, in which most of the increase in production came as a result of restoring and rehabilitating the existing production facilities left idle or partially destroyed during the Sino-Japanese war and the later civil war. The economic development since 1953 has had somewhat different characteristics in that the growth in production since then has taken place primarily

TABLE 1
CAPITAL INVESTMENT OF COMMUNIST CHINA
1952-1959

	Within & Outside the State Plan*			Within the State Plan		
	Total Investment (Million yuan)	Investment in Industry† (Million yuan)	Ratio	Total Investment (Million yuan)	Investment in Industry (Million yuan)	Ratio
1952	4,360	1,690	38.8%	3,710	1,549	41.7%
1953	8,000	2,840	35.4	6,510	2,756	42.4
1954	9,070	3,830	42.3	7,500	3,634	48.5
1955	9,300	4,300	46.2	8,630	4,204	51.2
1956	14,800	6,820	46.1	13,990	—	—
1957	13,830	7,240	52.3	12,640	—	—
1958	26,700	17,300	64.8	21,440	—	—
1959	31,700	—	—	26,700	—	—

Sources:

(1) All data for 1952-1958, except the figures for investment in industry within the state plan, are taken from TGY, pp. 55, 56, 59, and 61.

(2) For investment in industry within the state plan for 1952-1955, see SSB, "Economic Statistical Abstract," HHPYK, 1956, No. 17, p. 42.

(3) Figures for 1959 are from Li Hsien-Nien, "Report on the 1959 Final State Accounts and the Draft 1960 State Budget," JMJP, April 1, 1960.

* Investment outside the state plan is the investment made by local government and individual enterprises with their own funds.

† Industry, according to the official definition, includes manufacturing, mining, and electricity, but not geological survey or the prospecting of natural resources.

on the basis of new investment and new construction under the five year plans.

1952 is also the weighting year for this index. However, the weighting system is a hybrid one with wage bills as inter-industry weights and unit prices as intra-industry weights. The basic materials from which the weights are derived are again those officially published. Most of them became available in 1956 and 1957, a period known as "hundred flowers to bloom," when the flow of economic statistics was least restricted.

To utilize the official statistics as raw materials inevitably involves two serious difficulties. The first problem is the incompleteness of data. Not all the needed data are readily available and we must rely from time to time on our own estimates with unknown margins of error. Secondly, the question of reliability and accuracy may be raised in regard to the official statistics. To examine the whole problem in great detail would require separate research work. Our attempt in this study is to minimize the biases inherent in the official output index, biases due primarily to inappropriate methodology and malpractices in computing the official statistics at the aggregate level. But whenever it is necessary, attention will be drawn to the problematic points in the basic data used and readers will be forewarned about possible distortions and the limitations of the resulting indexes.

Unlike economic research work in most Western countries, for which the researcher can obtain the statistical data needed easily and systematically from a handful of sources, we have to collect data for our purpose from a great variety of widely scattered sources, including speeches, statements, and reports made by high-ranking officials; communiques of the State Statistical Bureau; editorials and feature articles of newspapers and periodicals; and pamphlets published by certain commercial fairs and exhibitions. In order to shorten the text as well as the footnotes contained in this study, all Communist Chinese publications are to be cited in abbreviated form and a list of the abbreviations is to be found at the end of the book.

Chapter II presents a brief discussion of the statistical logic of constructing an output index and a theoretical comparison of various types of output index formulae. We then proceed to scrutinize, in Chapter III, Communist China's official indexes of industrial output in order to see how far and why they may depart from what they are supposed to measure. Although issues are discussed from a methodological point of view, empirical information is furnished in each case to prove the existence of distortions and to indicate, where possible, their magnitude.

Chapter IV contains a detailed blueprint of the statistical procedures employed in constructing our new indexes and certain comments on the official data used as raw materials. This chapter is divided into two parts, one dealing with the weighting system and the other with the physical output series. The first part contains a thorough discussion of theoretical and practical reasons for which wage bills were used as inter-industry weights and prices as intra-industry weights.

Chapter V, the conclusion, analyses the implications which may be drawn from the resulting output indexes, and compares China's rates of industrial growth with those of other selected nations.

All the official data collected for the purpose of constructing our indexes are separately presented in the appendixes. Along with them are some technical notes concerning the derivation of our estimates for certain missing figures. They are so arranged that interested readers can easily inspect them and those who wish to make further use of them can conveniently do so.

CHAPTER II

Formulae of Production Indexes

An index of industrial production represents a series designed to measure changes over time in the volume of physical output[1] of the industrial sector of an economy. In constructing such an index a major task is that of combining, in a meaningful way, a number of measures of physical output of individual commodities produced[2] by various industries in each year in the period under study. More specifically, one first measures the movements of physical output for individual commodities and then aggregates them to show the quantity variation for the industrial sector as a whole by applying to the component series a set of weights. The weights, or the weighting system, used here will indicate the relative importance of the component series in their contributions to or influences on the quantity variation of total industrial production.

There are several weighting systems available for use, at least theoretically, in combining physical volume series, and each weighting system leads to a different formula with which a meaningful index of output can be calculated. The choice among alternative weighting systems, hence formulae, should be made not only on the basis of the comparative merits and demerits of each weighting system and its index formula, but also on the basis of the data available.

The most generally used type of weighting system in constructing an index of industrial production is value weights. That is to say, the relative importance of each included product is measured by its unit value in a given period. Since an overall index of industrial production is intended to reflect output changes at all stages of production within the industrial sector, we should measure, with no duplication, the net values added by all branches of industry. Consequently, the desired index number of a given period in relation to the base period is given by the following formula:[3]

$$\frac{\Sigma q_1 p_w - \Sigma Q_1 P_w}{\Sigma q_0 p_w - \Sigma Q_0 P_w} \qquad (1)$$

where Q and P stand for the quantities and the prices, respectively, of the materials and other commodities consumed in the production process; q and p represent the quantities and the prices, respectively, of finished products; the subscripts o and 1 indicate the two periods compared; and the subscript w indicates the period from which the value weights are taken.[4] In this formula, only the net output in a given year weighted by a set of prices is compared with the net output in the base year weighted by the same set of weights. It is free from any duplication or double-counting.

Alternatively, one may compute value added per unit of physical output for each commodity in the weighting period and use these value-added units as weights in aggregating the total industrial outputs in the two periods compared. Let V_w be the value added per unit of a given commodity in the weighting period, then $V_w = p_w - P_w Q_w/q_w$. And the index formula to be used is:

$$\frac{\Sigma q_1 V_w}{\Sigma q_0 V_w} \qquad (2)$$

V_w is the market price of the given commodity in the weighting period minus the value of materials and commodities consumed per unit of the finished commodity in the same period. This formula differs from (1) in that we calculate the value of materials and commodities consumed in the process of making a given product for only a single period, namely, the weighting period, and apply the unit net value so obtained to all periods under study. It is apparent that although this approach avoids the problem of double-counting in constructing an output index, it does not yield the same result as that obtained by using formula (1) unless

$$\frac{P_w Q_w}{q_w} = \frac{P_w Q_0}{q_0} = \frac{P_w Q_1}{q_1}$$

for each commodity, or changes in the cost structure for various commodities offset each other. This equality is not generally attained because with technological advancement the amount of materials consumed per unit of finished product tends to change for most industrial commodities and because some substitution between materials may take place in response to changes in the relative prices of different kinds of materials.

6

Formulae of Production Indexes

In order to compute an index of net physical output for the whole industrial sector one must know the physical quantities and prices not only of finished products but also of the commodities and materials consumed in the making of those finished products. This may be impracticable, or utterly impossible, in some cases owing to the inadequacy of data. In most countries data of value added are taken from the census of production, which may give values of net output only down to a certain level of the classification of industries. Below that level net output cannot be precisely calculated due to joint costs resulting from the prevalence of joint production. In this case, one is compelled to use gross values as weights. This alternative approach is the gross-value weights formula, represented algebraically by

$$\frac{\Sigma q_1 p_w}{\Sigma q_0 p_w} \qquad (3)$$

Here, only the finished products, q, enter into the formula; that is, we are comparing the quantities of the finished products of two periods, weighted by the same set of prices of those finished products, without substracting the values of commodities or materials used up in the process of production. This approach inevitably involves some double-counting or duplications. However, what really matters is not the double-counting itself but the degree of double-counting so imparted in the two periods compared. Formula (3) is not equal to (1) unless

$$\frac{\Sigma Q_1 P_w}{\Sigma q_1 p_w} = \frac{\Sigma Q_0 P_w}{\Sigma q_0 p_w}$$

In other words, these two formulae would yield identical results only when the degree of double-counting, as represented by $\Sigma Q P_w / \Sigma q p_w$, remains the same from the base year to the given year. As a rule, this equality is not attained if the index is aimed to measure changes in output for the industrial sector as a whole. Some industries consume more materials in their production than others and rates of changes in output over time for various industries are not likely to be identical; and their effects on the degree of double-counting are not likely to offset each other completely. However, this formula may be employed in constructing indexes for individual industries, each of which produces a single product with a single material or relatively homogeneous products with relatively homogeneous materials. In this case the discrepancy

7

between a gross-value index given by formula (3) and a net-value index given by formula (1) or (2) may not be serious and the former may be used as a good approximation to the latter two.

All weighting systems discussed above belong to the same general category, that is, value weights. There is another general group of weighting systems which differ from the value weights in that the weights are in non-value terms, such as labor requirement per unit of product or shipping tonnage per unit of product. Their application should be confined to cases where the index is to be constructed for some special purposes, or where the information necessary for value weights is limited or subject to serious distortion so that an index based on them becomes either infeasible or undesirable.

For some purposes, as during a period of emergency when transport is a limiting factor in the economy, shipment volume or weight of output is an important measure and may be taken as a weighting factor. The resulting formula is then

$$\frac{\Sigma q_1 t_w}{\Sigma q_0 t_w} \qquad (4)$$

where t_w represents the tonnage per unit of product measured in the weighting period.[5] The index so computed is a comparison of total shipping tonnages in different periods. Output changes of products which are relatively heavy but inexpensive would influence a tonnage measure more than a measure in dollar terms, so that this index often would give a result different from one based on value weights.

The second type of non-value weights which may be chosen to measure the relative importance of various industrial products, is labor requirements per unit of product in the weighting period. The resulting index formula is

$$\frac{\Sigma q_1 l_w}{\Sigma q_0 l_w} \qquad (5)$$

where l_w denotes labor requirements, usually in terms of man-hours per unit of product in the weighting period.[6]

An index obtained from this formula would differ from an index based on net-value weights because the degree of labor intensity, or the degree of capital intensity, varies from one industry to another. In other words, the ratio l_w/V_w is not identical for all commodities. This index, however, is important in the derivation of a productivity index.[7]

8

Another weighting system used in constructing output indexes is known as the wage-bill weights. To be more precise, the weights to be used are wage costs per unit of output for various commodities. Let r_w be the unit wage costs of a product in the weighting period; the index formula is then

$$\frac{\Sigma q_1 r_w}{\Sigma q_0 r_w} \tag{6}$$

Two different interpretations may be given to this wage-bill weighting system. For an economy where components other than wage costs in the net value contained in each commodity, or added by each industry branch, cannot be identified or estimated for some reason,[8] wage-bill weights may be used as an approximation to net-value weights. They are then considered as value weights. Alternatively, we may regard the wage-bill weights as modified labor-requirements weights. One of the shortcomings suffered by labor-requirements weights is that labor is assumed to be a homogeneous factor and man-hours are taken as the common measure of labor input in all industries without regard to differences in skill between various types of workers. Wage bills of various industries are, theoretically, labor requirements thoroughly weighted by degrees of skill of workers, as represented by differential wage rates. If looked at from this angle, wage-bill weights are nonvalue in nature, though they are stated in money terms.

The above listed formulae for output indexes are fixed-weights formulae, i.e. the Laspeyres or modified Laspeyres form. Each of them has a counterpart in the current-weights form, generally known as the Paasche formula, and in such modified Paasche formulae as the Fisher ideal formula, the Edgeworth-Marshall formula, and the chain index formula.[9]

Furthermore, all above-listed formulae are arithmetic means, or what is sometimes called linear aggregates. For each of them one may write some nonlinear formulae such as geometric means or harmonic means.

Statistically, all index formulae mentioned here are meaningful. For a binary comparison one may choose an index formula from this great variety; but when our task is to construct a series of index numbers for a large number of years, the choice of formulae and weights is much restricted. Here the choice really falls among various fixed-weights formulae and weighting periods, in view of the available data. That is to say, one may choose a fixed-weights

9

formula and decide whether the weights should be drawn from an early year or a late year or a combination of years in the period studied. The Paasche, the ideal, and the Edgeworth-Marshall formulae are virtually ruled out, because the current weights are usually not available. More often than not, an index maker will find that the real problem is to reconcile the theoretical principles of index-making with the practical necessity of using data which are incomplete and not on the desired basis. The nature of the available data may compel one to modify the procedure and construct what may be called a best "practicable index."

In actual computation, index formulae (2) through (6) can be transformed into their equivalent formulae which will tremendously reduce computational work yet yield the same results as would be obtained directly from the original formulae. Taking the gross-value weights formula for example, the working formula becomes:

$$\frac{\Sigma \frac{q_1}{q_0} q_0 p_w}{\Sigma q_0 p_w}$$

It can be easily seen that, mathematically, this formula is precisely equal to $\Sigma q_1 p_w / \Sigma q_0 p_w$. With the transformed formula one first converts all commodity series into quantity relatives, as expressed by q_1/q_0 and then applies $q_0 p_w$ as the weights to all relatives in a given year. This weighted relative expression, as it is sometimes called, of the original formula would reduce the computational work when an index is constructed for a number of years, because one has to calculate $q_0 p_w$ only once instead of computing $q_1 p_w$ for each year.

To sum up, in the absence of data needed to construct a net-value index (formula 1), an index maker may use any one of formulae 2 to 6 as an approximation. In doing so certain distortion would be introduced in the resulting index. The direction and magnitude of the distortion may vary, depending on the formula chosen, the changes over time in the product-mix, and changes in the cost structures in those industries. The problem is more serious for an economy undergoing rapid industrialization than for a mature economy. While no digression in this respect will be made here, some technical notes may be found in the Appendix A (pp. 105-16) discussing the possible effects of industrialization on various output indexes.

CHAPTER III

An Appraisal of the Official Indexes of Industrial Output of Communist China

Having examined what an index of industrial output is supposed to measure and how it should be constructed, one can make a critical appraisal of the official indexes of industrial output published by the Chinese Communists. This chapter is devoted to a detailed evaluation of official indexes to determine why and how these indexes misrepresent the true development of China's industrial production.

The official indexes of industrial output with various coverages and designations were published each year in the State Statistical Bureau's (SSB) annual communiques on the achievements of economic constructions and were brought together up to 1958 in *The Ten Great Years: Statistics of the Economic and Cultural Achievements of the People's Republic of China.*[1] They are shown in Table 2.

These official indexes of industrial output are considered to have various biases or errors. Here we intend to point out, very briefly, the proven biases and errors, and to try to minimize, if complete removal is impossible, these biases in our new indexes of industrial output.

The defects that can be found so far in the official indexes of industrial output in Communist China fall into three general categories: (1) biases due to the concept of gross value used by the Chinese Communists in making their indexes, (2) biases due to the peculiarities of their pricing practices, and (3) incomparability of the index numbers calculated for various years, stemming from the changed coverage.

1. Biases Due to the Gross-Value Concept Used

As we pointed out in the preceding chapter, an overall index of industrial output based entirely on gross values of output inevitably

11

TABLE 2
GROSS VALUE OF INDUSTRIAL OUTPUT IN COMMUNIST CHINA
1949-1959
(In Millions of Yuan)

Year	Whole Industry		Gross Output Value of Industry*				Gross Output Value of Factory Production		Gross Output Value of Handicrafts	
			Means of Production		Consumer Goods					
	(1) Value	(2) Index	(3) Value	(4) Index	(5) Value	(6) Index	(7) Value	(8) Index	(9) Value	(10) Index
At 1952 Prices										
1949	14,020	100.0	3,730	100.0	10,290	100.0	10,780	100.0	3,240	100.0
1950	19,120	136.4	5,650	151.6	13,470	130.8	14,060	130.4	5,060	156.4
1951	26,350	188.0	8,500	228.0	17,850	173.5	20,210	187.5	6,140	189.7
1952	34,330	244.9	12,220	327.8	22,110	214.8	27,020	250.6	7,310	225.9
1953	44,700	318.8	16,680	447.5	28,020	272.2	35,580	330.1	9,120	281.7
1954	51,970	370.8	19,990	536.3	31,980	310.8	41,510	385.1	10,460	323.1
1955	54,870	391.4	22,890	614.2	31,980	310.7	44,750	415.1	10,120	312.7
1956	70,360	501.9	32,040	859.7	38,320	372.4	58,660	544.2	11,700	361.5
1957	78,390	559.2	37,940	1020.0	40,450	393.0	65,020	603.2	13,370	412.9
At 1957 Prices										
1957	70,400		33,000		37,400					
1958	117,000	929.4	67,000	2070.0	50,000	525.4				
1959	163,000									

Sources:
1. All figures for 1949 to 1958 in columns (1) to (6), (9) and (10) are taken from *TGY*, pp. 87, 88, 91, and 94.
2. For 1959, Li Fu-chun, "Report on the Draft of National Economic Plan for 1960," *JMJP*, March 31, 1960.
3. In column (7), figures for 1949 and 1952 to 1955 are from *HHPYK*, 1956, No. 17, p. 40, figures for 1950, 1951, 1956, and 1957 are calculated by subtracting the figures in column (9) from those in (1) for each year; figures in column (8) are calculated from column (7).

* On p. 87 of *TGY*, it is not indicated whether the "gross output value of industry" includes "handicraft production." However, by comparing it with the figures and the related footnotes given by SSB in its annual reports one finds that it does include "handicraft production."

involves some double-counting. While the degree of double-counting may not vary seriously over a short period of time in the case of a mature economy whose industrial structure remains relatively stable, it might rise over time in an economy characterized by rapid industrialization. Presumably, most of the productive activities in the industrial sector of an underdeveloped country would be devoted to industries producing more raw materials than fabricated goods for export to exchange for finished goods produced abroad. But as large-scale industrialization is carried out, this economy would develop or establish more and more processing industries which would consume the materials domestically produced. The net result of this development might introduce an upward bias in the output index computed from gross values of industrial production. This has been largely the situation in Communist China in the past ten years or so.

To make things worse, the Chinese Communists do not calculate the aggregate gross value of industrial production by multiplying physical quantities of individual products by their unit prices, as expressed by Σqp in our index formula. Instead they have used a so-called "factory-reporting method"[2] in arriving at total gross value of industrial production for each year. Both the concept of and the computation method for the gross value of production are borrowed from Soviet Russia with little modification. The gross value of production reported by each individual enterprise is defined as the value of products, whether finished or semi-finished, turned out by this enterprise during the year, plus or minus any change in the amount of unfinished goods in process of production inside the enterprise over the year.[3] The aggregate gross value of total industrial production in each year is simply a summation of all the gross values reported by individual industrial enterprises in that year. Index numbers based on gross value so calculated are subject to the following distortions:

(a) Except in the ferrous metal, nonferrous metal, paper, and petroleum industries,[4] no double-counting within an enterprise is permitted, but inter-enterprise double-counting is permissible in computing gross value of production under the "factory-reporting method." In other words, raw materials produced and used up by the same enterprise must not be counted but all materials coming from outside the enterprise will enter in full value into the gross production figures. It is clear that the degree of double-counting existing in the aggregate gross value of industrial production as calculated from the formula Σqp is independent of the average degree of vertical integration of industrial enterprises in an economy. But the degree of double-counting in the calculation of aggregate gross value under the "factory-reporting method" is affected by the average degree of vertical integration of industrial enterprises. For instance, the total gross value of one bolt of colored cotton cloth and one bale of cotton yarn, if calculated from the formula Σqp, remains the same regardless of whether they are produced by two separate factories or by a single vertically integrated enterprise. This total gross value varies, however, if the "factory-reporting method" is employed, depending on the number of firms which contributed to producing them. If they are produced by the same enterprise, the value of colored cotton cloth would be counted; if one plant produced the cotton yarn and another wove and dyed the cloth, then both the value of the yarn and the value of the cloth would be counted; if one plant produced cotton yarn, another wove cloth and a third plant dyed it, then the value of the cotton yarn would be counted three times and the value of the undyed cloth twice.

In principle we know then that the degree of double-counting introduced into the aggregate gross value of industrial production in Communist China is subject to a greater variability due to their peculiar way of computing. It is not always clear, however, in which direction and to what extent their indexes of industrial output are biased solely from this factor.

From Table 3 one can see that the total number of producing units in the industrial sector of Communist China remained very stable prior to 1955, but declined sharply in 1955 and 1956. The diminution in the number of the industrial establishments in those two years was, apparently, the result of mergers, vertical as well as horizontal, among enterprises, and of the absorption of private firms by the state-owned enterprises under the vigorous campaign of socialization during this period. This could have given, to a certain extent, a downward bias to the official output indexes. But the situation became quite different after 1958. In that year a huge number of small plants and factories were formed in urban areas as well as in the people's communes, as a result of the movement of "walking with two legs." One Communist source reports that 75,000,000 new industrial units were established in Mainland China during the short period from January to September of 1958, among them more than 6,000,000 units belonging to the agricultural

14

Official Indexes of Industrial Output

TABLE 3
NUMBER OF INDUSTRIAL ESTABLISHMENTS IN COMMUNIST CHINA

Year	Total	Large-scale	Small-scale
1952	167,402	27,527	139,876
1953	176,405	31,379	145,026
1954	167,626	31,187	136,439
1955	125,474		
1956	60,000		

Sources:
1. For 1952 to 1955, State Statistical Bureau, "Economic Statistical Abstract," *HHPYK*, No. 17, Sept. 1956, p. 40.
2. For 1956, Wang Ssu-hua, "The Actual Functions of Statistics in Our Economic Construction and Problems Concerning Some Indicators," *CCYC*, No. 5, May 1958, p. 29.

Note:
Not all of those industrial establishments were independent accounting units. According to Wang Ssu-hua, only 40,000 out of the 60,000 enterprises in 1956 had independent accounting systems. See Wang Ssu-hua, *ibid.*

cooperatives and the people's communes.[5] The number of new industrial concerns established in the first nine months of 1958 is 125 times the total number of industrial establishments existing in 1956. All these newly formed small plants and factories engaged in only one-stage production with simple native methods. It is beyond doubt that this development tremendously reduced the average degree of vertical integration in the industrial structure, and hence significantly exaggerated rates of growth, as shown by official indices, of industrial output for the years since 1958.

(b) As indicated above, the provisions governing methods of calculation and compilation of industrial statistics permit double-counting within some enterprises of certain goods produced and consumed by the concern. They are:[6]

(1) Iron ore, fireproof materials, coke and its by-products, steel ingots, and other steel products produced and consumed by the same iron and steel mill.

(2) Metal ore produced and consumed by nonferrous metallurgical mills.

(3) Pulp produced and consumed by the same paper-manufacturing plant.

(4) Petroleum products extracted and consumed by the same petroleum enterprise.

These special provisions would presumably exaggerate production values for these four industries relative to other industries. Their relatively high rates of growth must have given an upward bias to official indexes over a period of time by raising the general degree of double-counting for the industrial sector as a whole.

(c) Another bias arising from their method of computing the gross value of production stems from the fact that individual enterprises may use certain devices to exaggerate their gross value figures. Since gross value of production is one of the most important indicators of the success of any enterprise in Communist China, there is strong incentive for managerial and operating personnel to embellish achievement by exaggerating gross value figures. One way of doing this is to increase the production of those commodities which are more material-consuming. In fact, this has been a common practice in some factories, especially in local industries which have greater freedom in choosing products to be manufactured.[7] In enterprises having less freedom to choose their own output, producers have been inclined to select the most expensive raw materials for their products.[8] A factory facing a possible failure to fulfill the target assigned to it might rescue itself by sending out its materials to other firms, usually private industries, for partial processing, and taking them back to finish the final process itself. As long as it performed the final process of production the value of the final products would be legally counted as part of its gross value of production.[9] This practice has been carried out to the extreme in one case in which two textile factories exchanged their outputs of undyed cotton cloth for the dying process, thus reported gross values of production for both factories were almost double what they would otherwise have been.[10] These many distortions stemming from the defective reporting system may not be classified as "falsification" in the sense of maintaining a double bookkeeping system, but, nevertheless, they contribute to the increased degree of double-counting embodied in the official figures for gross value.

(d) There is another type of distortion attributable to "factory-reporting method" of computing gross value. The gross values of industrial output reported by individual enterprises may sometimes include the values of non-industrial products either because producers desire to write up their gross value figures or because of the practical difficulty of separating industrial from non-industrial products when the reporting enterprises are engaging at the same time in both types of activity. A typical example is given in the following statement quoted from a Communist source regarding the chemical industry.

In the value index of the chemical industry production, basic and non-basic as well as some non-chemical products were included. For instance, according to the regulations of the State Statistical Bureau, granular fertilizer and bacterial fertilizer should not be included in the statistics of chemical fertilizer; and any vegetable agricultural insecticide made by simple methods (such as the water-soaking method) should not be considered as chemical insecticides. Such regulations are essential and correct. However, when the chemical production value index is computed, these fertilizers and insecticides are all included. At the present time, the value of non-chemical products included in the index cannot be accurately estimated, but a rough estimate shows that 46% of the total value of the fertilizer industry in 1958 was of non-chemical fertilizer.[11]

This phenomenon is believed to have been serious and most common in 1958 when all enterprises in Communist China were faced with strong pressure to fulfill or overfulfill their targets under the so-called "great leap forward" campaign.

2. *Biases Due to the Peculiarities of the Price Structure*

For the Soviet-type economy in general, objections may be raised against using a value-weights index to measure changes in physical output because of the questionable significance of prices in such an economy. The value weights, net or gross, are either unit prices themselves or derived from prices according to a certain formula. In a free-enterprise economy prices do represent scarcity relationships among various commodities, but in an economy where the market mechanism ceases to function and commodity prices are largely determined by planners' decisions, prices need not signify the relative importance of various commodities.

For Communist China in particular, the use of prices as weights in constructing the gross value index of industrial output suffers from certain specific shortcomings:

(a) Official indexes of industrial output for the years prior to 1957 were computed on the basis of 1952 constant prices, or more specifically, the weighted average prices during the third quarter of that year. The "Five-Anti" campaign against private industry and trade in 1952 seriously depressed prices of consumer goods but had little effect on prices of producer goods. Therefore,

17

the 1952 constant prices represent a pattern in which producer goods were over-priced in relation to consumer's goods. This has given unduly high weight to producers' goods which have had in general a greater rate of growth than consumers' goods. The upward bias so introduced into the official output values is by no means insignificant, though we cannot tell the exact extent of it. In fact, the overpricing of producers' goods has been admitted and criticized by a number of Chinese Communist writers, including some responsible economists in the Central Planning Commission.[12] A Communist economist revealed on one occasion that before 1956 the average profit-cost ratio for all heavy industries had always been above 50%, and that, after the price of steel was cut by 30% in 1956, the profit-cost ratio of Anshan Iron & Steel Works was still as high as 120%.[13] Although the then current internal-transfer prices of some producers' goods were lowered in 1955 and 1956,[14] the constant prices used in computing the gross value index were not altered until 1957. A new set of constant prices were calculated in 1957 and made effective for use beginning January 1, 1958. They are weighted average prices for January 1, 1957. The level of the new constant prices for all industrial products was 10.2% lower than that of the 1952 constant prices, and 13.1% and 7.6% lower for producers' goods and consumers' goods respectively.[15] It is difficult to tell whether the overpricing of producers' goods has been completely corrected through this 1957 adjustment of constant prices. We are certain, however, that value figures for industrial production before 1957 were exaggerated because of this factor.

(b) The second upward-biasing factor under this general category involves prices of new products whose production began after 1952. According to provision set forth by the State Statistical Bureau constant prices of new products appearing after 1952 were obtained by deflating their first factory-prices with some conversion coefficients calculated from price movements of similar products between 1952 and the year when the new product appeared.[16] The problem centers on how the first factory-price was determined when a new product became available for sale. According to one Communist source, trial-manufacturing expenses or costs of any new industrial product were to be allocated only to the first year of production, and the factory-price in the first year was fixed by marking up 5% to 15% profits on total trial-manufacturing costs.[17] As a rule, the trial-manufacturing costs of any

18

new product and thus the first factory-price so determined would be much higher than the prices of the existing similar products, from which the conversion coefficient was computed. The constant prices applying to new products, as computed in this manner, would undoubtedly give unduly high weights to them. Again, these overweighted items are exactly the items which have greater growth rates simply because they are new.[18]

(c) New industrial products were not the only category whose constant prices were not readily available. Two other groups of products have encountered the same problem: (1) so-called "non-principal products" and some outputs manufactured by local industries, which were not distributed by the central or provincial governments, and (2) products made by private industries prior to 1957.

In view of the practical difficulties involved, the central planning authority in Communist China gave freedom to local state enterprises in determining constant prices for their products which were less important and highly heterogeneous in kind. According to regulations, those prices should have been set according to factory prices in 1952 and remained constant thereafter. But, in fact, most local industries have set their constant prices much higher than this. The high constant prices enabled these factories to fulfill their production targets easily in terms of gross values, yet they sold their products at current prices which were lower than constant prices. This situation has been clearly pointed out by one Communist writer in regard to chemical products:

> The 'constant prices' of non-principal products are usually too high. According to the regulations of selecting a constant price, the State Statistical Bureau and the Ministry of Chemical Industry determine only the prices of principal items; prices of many non-principal items are fixed by the industries themselves based on factory prices. In general, prices of those non-principal items which are not distributed by the central government or provincial governments are usually fixed too high, therefore the fixed prices used in the calculation of the production value of these items are also too high. . . . Some of the prices fixed by the plants themselves may be several times as high as their original costs and even several times as high as the current market prices.[19]

On another occasion, one Communist writer gave an empirical

comparison of 1952 constant prices and current prices of selected machinery products manufactured by local industries. This writer did not mention when these current prices were quoted, nor did he make clear on what basis this sample was drawn. Unlike the

TABLE 4
CONSTANT PRICES AND CURRENT PRICES FOR SELECTED MACHINERY PRODUCTS
OF LOCAL INDUSTRIES (IN YUAN)

Item	1952 Constant Price	Current Price
Sewing Machine	190.00	108.60
8" Water Pumps	1,590.00	424.00
Tip Cart	6,583.70	6,400.00
Sprayer	28.40	20.00
Threshing Machine	90.30	66.00
51 Type Plow	25.00	15.81
Cultivator	7.80	9.80

Source:
    Lo Chin-hua, "A Problem of Using the Gross Value to Check the Production Plan in the Local Machinery Industries," *TCKT*, No. 4, Feb. 1957, p. 6.

case of new products, the direction of the bias introduced by this factor alone into the over-all indexes of industrial production cannot be determined because we do not know whether the items produced by local industries have had relatively greater growth rates.

    The field of private industries was another in which the value of production was not computed at 1952 constant prices. Each private enterprise was required to calculate its own monthly production figures valued at prices for the 15th day of the month. Annual production was simply a summation of all monthly figures for the year. After all production figures for private firms in a region were collected and aggregated by the regional office in charge of private enterprises, a uniform deflator or conversion coefficient was applied to convert the aggregate gross value of private production in a given period into an equivalent in terms of 1952 constant prices. Some distortions would be created under this indirect method of computation, but the extent and the direction of the distortions are not clear.[20] This complication disappeared after practically all private industries were socialized in 1956.

    (d) As we have pointed out, the official indexes of industrial output up to 1957 were computed on the basis of 1952 constant prices, while the indexes since 1958 are based on 1957 constant prices. However, no attempt has been made to recalculate index numbers before 1958 on the basis of the new set of constant prices to make series in the two periods comparable. Not even a benchmark index has been made for the earlier years on the basis of the new prices. The difficulty is understandable. The "factory-reporting method" makes this recalculation impossible. The State Statistical Bureau simply calculated the gross value of industrial production for 1957 twice—once at 1952 constant prices and once at 1957 constant prices—and uses them as a link connecting the two series of index numbers, before and after 1957, with 1949 (or 1952) remaining as the base year.[21]

3. The Incomparability of Coverage

The last type of distortion which is by far the most serious and inexcusable from a statistical point of view is the incomparability of index numbers for various periods resulting from changed coverage. Although the fact that the Communist authorities have presented some incomparable index numbers without explicitly indicating the changes in coverage may not be properly classified as "falsification," their deliberate intention to mislead the reader is transparently clear.

(a) Evidence shows that the official definition of the industrial sector in Communist China has been broadened in the past decade to include some products which previously belonged to other sectors. A typical example is that of aquatic products.[22] Prior to May 12, 1956, there was no separate ministry in the central government responsible for the production of aquatic output. At the national level it belonged to the Ministry of Agriculture, and for a very short period to the Ministry of Commerce.[23] At the local level the classification was even more confusing. Aquatic production could fall under the jurisdiction of the agriculture departments, or the commerce departments, or the so-called "city services" departments of the local governments, depending on the administrative setup of various districts.[24] All 1,570,000 able-bodied fishermen out of the estimated 4,570,000 fishery population were considered as primary producers of aquatic products.[25] All official documents on the First Five Year Plan released after 1955 and the SSB's annual communiques for 1955 and 1956 classified aquatic production as a part of agriculture activities.[26]

An independent Ministry of Aquatic Production was first formed in the central government on May 12, 1956; but aquatic output was not counted as a part of industrial production until some time in 1958. In Po-I-po's "Draft Plan for the Development of the National Economy in 1958" (announced on February 14, 1958) the production of aquatic products was for the first time included in light industry. In *TGY*, which was compiled and first published in September 1959, aquatic products appeared in the list of major industrial commodities produced in Communist China.[27] Moreover, since then only the workers and employees of the state-owned fishing or fish-breeding enterprises and processing factories have been classified as industrial workers in aquatic production.[28]

Timber production presents a less clear case. It belonged to the Ministry of Forestry (called the Ministry of Forestry and Cultivation in 1949 and 1950) whose activities were agricultural in nature. A separate Ministry of Forest Industry was established on May 12, 1956, to take care of timber production and related activities. However, it has never been made clear to the public by the Communist authorities whether the value of the timber industry's output has been counted as part of the gross value of industrial output only since the establishment of the Ministry of Forest Industry or from the beginning of the regime. The timber industry was listed as one of the branches of heavy industry in the First Five Year Plan released in 1955, and its production figures for the 1952 and 1957 planned targets were accordingly reported.[29] But it is not clear whether the output value of timber was actually counted as part of the gross value of total industrial production when lumbering activities were administratively subject to the control of a non-industrial organization before the release of the First Five Year Plan in 1955 or before the establishment of the independent Ministry of Forest Industry in 1956.

The pertinent question is not whether the definition of industry should be so broadened but whether the gross values of industrial output in earlier years have been adjusted in accordance with the broadened coverage in making the official output indexes. Apparently, the Chinese Communists have not made these adjustments. The following table (Table 5) shows various gross value figures of industrial output. All data were published in 1956. A comparison of these figures with columns (1) and (9) in Table 2, will show that they are the same as the figures given in *TGY*, which was published in late 1959; and all the slight differences are merely the result of rounding off. This means that the official index numbers of gross output values as presented in *TGY* are not comparable because gross output values for the years before 1958, which are identical with the figures in Table 5, do not include aquatic products while gross output values since 1958 include aquatic products.

TABLE 5

GROSS VALUE OF INDUSTRIAL OUTPUT AT 1952 PRICES, 1949-1955

(in Million Yuan)

Year	All Industry	Industry Exclusive of Handicrafts			Handicraft Production
		Total	Modern Industry	Handicrafts Factory	
1949	14,018	10,781	7,913	2,868	3,237
1952	34,326	27,014	22,049	4,965	7,312
1953	44,696	35,577	28,809	6,768	9,119
1954	51,975	41,513	33,986	7,527	10,462
1955	54,871	44,748	37,082	7,666	10,123

Source:
SSB, "Economic Statistical Abstract," *HHPYK*, No. 17, Sept. 1956, p. 39.

(b) Handicraft production creates a unique problem for the official indexes. Presented here is a very brief description of the nature of this complication; a detailed discussion of the problem will be given in the next chapter. Handicraft production, as defined by SSB, comprises all products turned out by individual and cooperatively organized handicraftsmen, but excludes output from factories which employ handicraft methods of production. Owing to a variety of practical difficulties, statistical data concerning the value of production and other economic indicators of handicraft production are not collected from the reports submitted by producing units. Instead, general or sample surveys are conducted periodically by SSB; the information so gathered is far from complete and is less accurate than the data on factory production.[30] Therefore an output index exclusive of handicraft production is superior to one including it. Though gradual transformation of the handicraft industry had taken place in the early years of the Communist Regime, it was in 1958 that practically all remaining handicraftsmen, as individual operators or in cooperatives, were suddenly socialized. It was expected that practically all remaining handicraftsmen would be transferred either into state or commune factories.[31] The general impact of these factors on the output indexes are: (1) The quality of all official output data since 1958

23

has greatly deteriorated because of the inclusion of handicraft production, and (2) part of the increase in factory production in 1958 merely reflects the shift of former handicraft production into factory production. In other words, values of factory production before and since 1958 are not comparable as a result of the drastic change in social structure taking place during that year, though the official definition of factory production has remained unchanged.

CHAPTER IV

The Construction of New Indexes

It is clear that the need for a new index to measure changes in physical output of the industrial sector in Communist China is undisputed. The pertinent problem is not the selection of an ideal index according to the statistical logic of index making but how to reconcile the underlying statistical logic and the fundamental concepts with the available data which are both incomplete in quantity and ambiguous in meaning. We hope that, with improved methodology, the resulting new indexes will minimize the identified biases in the official indexes. The new indexes are to be constructed, therefore, along the following lines.

(1) Commodity series in physical terms should be used as the basis of the new indexes. First of all, this will avoid some biases found in the official indexes, such as that introduced by the varying degree of double-counting resulting from changes in the degree of vertical integration of industrial enterprises. The use of commodity series also eliminates certain biases arising from the "factory-reporting method." Furthermore, once the commodities, if clearly defined, are selected, the coverage of the output index remains constant throughout the whole period no matter how frequently the official classification of industry is altered.[1]

(2) Constant weights are to be devised. They should enable us to measure, approximately, if not precisely, the relative importance of the net contributions made by various industries to aggregate industrial output. Such weights should be least handicapped by the ambiguity resulting from the price structure in Communist China's economy.

This chapter is devoted to an explanation of, and comments on, the weighting system and the product series used in constructing our new indexes.

Rate and Pattern of Industrial Growth in Communist China

1. The Weights

A. INTRODUCTION

The critical problems involved in selecting weights for the construction of output indexes for Communist China are the following: (1) What type of weights is preferable or least unsatisfactory? (2) For a given type of weights, what time period should be chosen as the weighting period so that known biases can be minimized? In a Soviet-type economy, where the market mechanism ceases to function and prices are arbitrarily determined by planners, there is no *a priori* reason why value weights, net or gross, are superior to nonvalue weights, since value weights in this case may not necessarily reflect the relative importance of the output components. Several alternative methods of weighting have been tried in studies of industrial production in the Soviet economy in the hope of avoiding the ambiguity of domestic prices or value coefficients in general. However, no generalized conclusion has been reached concerning the selection of an appropriate weighting system in this situation. The research and experiments made in Soviet studies are far from sufficient to afford adequate empirical evidence for selecting a single weighting system generally applicable to all Communist countries. In most instances the choice is largely dictated by practical considerations such as those of data deficiencies and the institutional peculiarities existing in the society concerned.

One approach is an outright abandonment of value weights and use of nonvalue indicators. Some Western economists have attempted to measure Soviet industrial growth by using indicators such as consumption of minerals, fuels, steel, electric power and freight transportation volume.[2] However, in those studies nonvalue measures are used not as explicit weights, but as direct indicators or estimators of Soviet industrial growth. The obvious advantage of this method is that it avoids the difficulties of interpreting the significance of domestic prices in a planned economy; but it has disadvantages of its own, which may offset or more than offset its advantage.

Owing to the fact that the difficulties of securing nonvalue data usable as weights in Communist countries are even more formidable than the problem of collecting value weights, no Western economist has been able to construct an output index for any Communist country purely based on nonvalue weights. Several attempts have been made, however, to utilize nonvalue data as partial weights. The German Institute for Business Research published in 1940 an index of Soviet industrial output[3] computed on the basis of 47 quantity series weighted by (1) fixed capital invested in the individual branches of industry as of January 1, 1933 and (2) the size of the labor force in each branch in 1933, which is a nonvalue weight. Professor Nutter has measured Soviet industrial growth with 1955 employment figures as partial weights.[4]

An alternative approach to this problem is to make use of world market prices or prices in some other economy, say, that of the United States. A typical example is the Soviet industrial output index computed by Colin Clark for the years 1913 and 1921-1940, which weights product series by so-called "International Units," that is, average dollar prices of 1925-1934.[5] On a similar basis Alexander Gerschenkron has constructed first an index of the Soviet machinery industry during the period of 1927-28 to 1937 and later on an index of all heavy industry for the same period.[6] In his index, Professor Gerschenkron used 1939 U.S. prices for similar products turned out by the Soviet industry. Though computing this type of index for a Communist country makes direct international comparison possible, it is usually objected to on the ground that the prices or value weights taken from outside may not reflect relative scarcities in the country for which the production index is constructed.

Another alternative, which is generally considered more acceptable than the two methods just mentioned, is to use actual wage bills as weights. The credit for first employing wage-bill weights goes to Donald R. Hodgman who used them to construct an index of Soviet industrial production covering a period from 1928 to 1951.[7] Wage-bill weights may be viewed as a variation of labor-requirements weights. One of the shortcomings in using labor-requirements weights is that labor is assumed to be a homogeneous factor and man-hours are taken as the common measurement of labor inputs in all industries, disregarding differences in skill between various types of workers. Wage bills, with a more or less rational wage structure, represent the labor requirements of various industries thoroughly weighted by the degrees of skill of all workers. If looked at from this angle, wage-bill weights are improved labor-requirements weights. They eliminate some of the shortcomings of a nonvalue weighting system.

Wage-bill weights may be considered as an approximation to

net-value or value-added weights in a Communist economy or any economy where genuine value-added weights cannot be obtained. Value added in an industry, which is factor income originating in that industry, comprises wages and salaries, profits, interest, and rent. Among these, "wages and salaries" is the least ambiguous and the only identifiable item under the institutional setting of a Soviet-type economy.

In most Communist countries the means of industrial production are owned by the state. Consequently, "rent" and "interest" as separate categories of factor income have become unidentifiable. State banks may charge some nominal interest on working capital borrowed by various enterprises merely as a device to penalize those enterprises which have retained borrowed funds too long. It in no sense represents a return to capital.

More ambiguous is the category of "profits." Taking all state enterprises as a whole, aggregate profit is a sort of net monopolistic revenue and can hardly be distinguished conceptually from other forms of business taxes collected by the state.[8] For an individual state-enterprise, profit is merely the difference between the price of its product arbitrarily determined by the planners and the actual production cost which consists of costs of labor, raw materials, fuel and power, and the so-called "administration cost." Both the ratio of profits to production costs and ratio of profits to the total value of fixed capital vary tremendously from industry to industry, from one enterprise to another in the same industry, and from region to region, because of the arbitrariness of product prices and differential costs in various cases. Therefore, the category of "salaries and wages" is the only one in a Communist country that is clearly defined and conceptually similar to that in a free market economy.

Wage bills will be used as weights in this study. However, data deficiencies enable us to use wage-bill weights only where dealing with relatively broad categories of production. We are forced to use another type of weights, namely unit prices of products for breakdowns within broad industry classes. In fact this difficulty exists in constructing virtually all production indexes regardless of type of economy for which the index is constructed. This unconquerable obstacle arises from the common phenomenon of joint costs in production in all modern economies. Sooner or later an index maker finds it impossible to assign net value weights, whatever they are, to commodities broken down below a certain level of industrial classification. One way of tackling this problem is to break down the output series just to the level where information for calculating net output is available, and ignore sub-divisions below that level. An alternative way of dealing with this difficulty is to make use of other types of weights in the lower levels of classification where net value figures are not obtainable. The measure most commonly used at present is price, i.e., the unit gross value of each commodity, because price data are readily available (at least in most free states where no economic information is deliberately withheld) no matter how far one breaks down the output series.

Another justification for using prices as weights within industries is that if the scope of the industry is defined narrowly enough, the degree of double-counting resulting from the use of gross value weights in aggregating tends to be fairly stable, hence the gross value index constructed for this single industry may not depart very much from its true value-added index.

For example, in the revised Federal Reserve index of industrial production for the United States, value added in the manufacture of individual products has been estimated in most instances under the general assumption that value added is proportional to gross value, and the value added reported by Census for each industry has been distributed among the component product series on this basis.[9] This treatment has simplified the actual computation of an over-all output index because the index maker can directly calculate it from the individual product series instead of doing it in two stages, first applying the gross value weights to each component commodity to get the index numbers for various industries separately, and then applying the value-added weights among various industries to arrive at an overall index. This treatment does not change, however, the hybrid nature of its weighting system. Conceptually, the assumption that value added is proportional to gross value for each individual product amounts to the same thing as the direct use of gross value weights.

In summary, the use of gross values as intra-industry weights is a necessity common to all output indexes. The real difference among them is a matter of degree, varying according to the level of industrial classification at which gross value weights must be introduced.

Rate and Pattern of Industrial Growth in Communist China

Although commodity prices in a Communist country may not reflect the economy's true scarcity relationships, this fact becomes a less serious problem if prices are used only as weights within a narrowly defined industry or for a group of similar commodities. In most instances, commodities produced by a narrowly defined industry are close substitutes for one another and their prices must be related, even in a Communist country, in such a way that they roughly correspond to the relative satisfaction that users derive from these goods. For example, printed cloth and white cloth are close substitutes for each other; even silk or woolen fabrics are more or less substitutable for cotton cloth. In theory, if no reasonable relative prices are maintained among these commodities serious dislocations must take place in the absence of a strict rationing system. In fact, Communist planners in China did pay great attention to possible substitution between similar products, not only by consumers but also by the state enterprises, and to the problems which arise from unreasonable relative prices.[10]

Both the wage bills and prices used in this study are those for 1952. This weighting period is chosen for a number of reasons. By 1952 the war-torn economy on the China Mainland was for the first time restored to normal conditions after a long period of confusion and disorganization. More important the prolonged hyperinflation was slowed down and finally stopped in 1951. It is fairly safe to say that market psychology in 1952 was no longer inflation-oriented.

The year 1952 also has certain other advantages over later years as a weighting period. In early 1952 the vigorous campaign of transforming private enterprises into socialist or semi-socialist forms of organization had not yet begun. Until late 1952, a major economic policy of the Chinese Communist government encouraged businessmen to make new investment and enlarge production in the private sector. The important role of the private sector in the whole economy in 1952 favors taking price and wage-bill weights from that year instead of from any later year. Table 6 shows that the share of private industry in the whole industrial sector, taken either in terms of number of enterprises or in terms of gross value of production, was greater in 1952 than in later years.

Among thirteen industries included in our index, eight require intra-industry weights—the ferrous metal, metal processing, chemical, building materials, textile, paper, food, and daily-use commodities industries.

The Construction of New Indexes

TABLE 6
The Share of Private Industry in the Whole Industrial
Sector in Communist China, 1952-1955

	1952	1953	1954	1955
Number of private enterprises as a percentage of total industrial establishments	89.3	85.1	79.9	70.7
Gross output of private enterprises as a percentage of total gross value of factory production	39.0	36.8	24.9	16.0

Sources:
The shares of private industry in terms of number of enterprises are calculated from the numbers of private industrial enterprises as given in CN, p. 8 and the numbers of all industrial establishments in Table 5. Shares in terms of gross output value are given in CN, pp. 28 and 88.

Fortunately, in most of these eight industries private production as a percent of total production was fairly high in 1952, as Table 7

TABLE 7
Gross Value of Private Production as A Percentage of
Total Production in 1952, by Industry

Industry	Percentage
1. Electric power	7.8
2. Coal	8.0
3. Petroleum	0
4. Ferrous metal	9.6
5. Nonferrous metal	21.4
6. Metal processing	32.9
7. Chemical	36.7
8. Building materials	n.a.
9. Timber	n.a.
10. Textile	51.3
11. Paper	25.5
12. Food	n.a.
13. Daily-use commodities	n.a.
All industry	39.0

Sources:
For 1, 2, 4, 6, 10, and 11, from CH p. 71, p. 99, p. 13, p. 131, p. 176 and p. 213 respectively. For 5 and 7, the gross values of private production are given in CN, p. 89. The gross values of total production of these two industries are taken from Table 16. For 3, it was completely state-owned from the very beginning of this regime. See Economic Yearbook, Hong Kong, 1951, p. 44 and FFYP, p. 53.
For all industry, from HCKTKY, p. 66.

Rate and Pattern of Industrial Growth in Communist China

shows. Although no exact percentage is available for building materials, food, and daily-use commodities industries, their proportions of private production were roughly estimated by one Communist

TABLE 8
PRIVATE PRODUCTION AS A PERCENTAGE OF TOTAL
PRODUCTION IN 1952, BY COMMODITY

Item	Percentage
Coal	12
Caustic Soda	33
Cement	27
Electric Motors	21
Metal Cutting Machines	53
Cotton Yarn	37
Cotton Cloth	49
Paper	35
Matches	45
Rubber Footwear	53
Edible Oil	48
Flour	46
Cigarettes	29

Source:
JMJP, March 21, 1956.

writer to be more than 50% in 1952.[11] The only exception among the eight is the ferrous metal industry in which only 9.6% of its total production was turned out by private enterprises in 1952.

A similar picture can be seen from the percentages of private production to total production of major commodities, as shown in Table 8. As long as private firms as a whole still played a role as competitor with the public enterprises, the Communist authorities could not utterly ignore, when setting prices for the goods produced by state enterprises, the market prices in the private sector.

It should be noted, however, that the prices we have taken as intra-industry weights differ from the official 1952 constant prices in one very important respect. Our prices are those of January 1, 1952, while the official constant prices were computed from average prices for the third quarter of that year. The two sets of prices are drastically different because of the nation-wide "Five Anti" campaign initiated in mid-January of 1952 and concluded sometime in the third quarter of that year.[12] This was the first serious attempt since the establishment of the Chinese Communist regime to oppress ruthlessly private enterprise throughout the country. The first half of 1952 saw a serious drop in commodity prices in most urban centers in China.

The year 1952 is also a good choice for deriving wage-bill weights due to certain features of the labor market.

(1) Labor was not rigorously controlled in China until late 1954. Labor unions, which were designed primarily to control workers and not as collective bargaining organizations, grew rapidly in size only after 1952. The Ministry of Labor and its local agencies, which became important labor control agencies in later years, functioned in the first few years of the regime primarily as an arbitrator of disputes between workers and private employers.[13] Also, individual state enterprises had considerable freedom in hiring and dismissing workers in the period before 1954.[14] Another sign of the free labor market prevailing in 1952 was the high rate of turnover of labor, especially among skilled workers.[15]

After 1954, control over the labor market was tightened through a succession of new labor laws or decrees. In July 1954, the "Outline of Labor Regulations for State-Operated Enterprises" was promulgated. This new labor law provided various strict regulations concerning the employment, transfer and dismissal of workers and staff members in state enterprises.[16] Freedom of state enterprises in employing workers was further restricted in mid-1955 when the central government issued a decree forbidding the free hiring of workers by individual state enterprises. Any addition to the regular working staff in an enterprise had to be approved in advance by its superior organization or the Ministry of Labor.[17] Toward the end of 1957, another regulation was put into effect to control the use of "casual workers" in state enterprises.[18]

(2) According to official statements, the Communist government in Peking had a wage policy in 1952 which still showed some regard for labor preferences based on disutility and for shortages of skilled labor of various types. An eight-or-seven-grade wage system was first adopted in 1949 in the Northeastern area and was gradually extended throughout the country.[19] This wage system was intended to eliminate the idea of "equalitarianism" and the "principle of using wages as a means of relief,"[20] both of which prevailed in the wage system in the "old liberated area" prior to 1948 but which were by 1949 regarded as undesirable or harmful to modern industry from an incentive point of view. It was said that the eight-or-seven-grade wage system provided sufficient material incentives to workers by setting large wage differentials between grades and among different types of work and different industries. While minimum wages for the lowest grade workers and the differ-

entials between successive grades were set by the wage law for each industry individually according to general skill requirements in that industry, classification of the individual worker was made within the enterprise by considering such factors as the requisite technical skill, the degree of responsibility, the degree of exertion, and working conditions.

The intention of the Communist authorities to structure wages so that compensation reflected disutilities among various types of work was also shown in their effort to spread the piece-rate wage system and the system of paying bonuses to workers who had over-fulfilled their work quotas.[21] However, due to some practical difficulties, the authorities had never been very successful in promoting the piece-rate wage system in the industrial sector.

Prior to 1954, the wage system in Communist China might have served, to some extent, as a means of allocating labor resources among various industries. Beginning in 1954, labor mobility was restricted and the allocation of labor became more or less independent of the wage mechanism, but, this direct government control over labor did not necessarily mean that the principle of setting wage rates to reflect the disutility of work was discarded.

(3) The 1952 wage bills are preferred to those of any later year because the proportion of employment by private enterprises in total employment in the industrial sector was higher in 1952 than in later years. It was 47.1% in 1952. The proportion of private employment was as high as 54.9% in 1952 if both industry and commerce are taken together.[22]

B. WAGE BILLS

The wage bill for each industry is computed by multiplying its employment figure for 1952 by the average 1952 wage rate in that industry. In doing this, two conceptual problems are encountered: What employment figures should be taken, and what wage rate should be used?

Industrial concerns in Communist China usually do not confine their activities to the production of industrial commodities. One often finds that an industrial enterprise embraces some subordinate units engaging in construction which is excluded from the coverage of our index, or in running agricultural, pasture, laundry, mess hall, nursery and other nonindustrial works. Moreover, there are fairly numerous political personnel in practically every productive estab-

34

lishment, whose work is much broader in scope than that of so-called "public relations" or "labor relations" offices in firms in the Western world. The distinction between real industrial workers and other personnel in their contributions to industrial production is fully recognized by the Communists themselves. Consequently employment figures reported by individual enterprises are officially divided into two categories as indicated below:[23]

(1) Industrial productive personnel: This category comprises all workers and employees who directly participate in productive activities and those whose services are required in the productive process. Specifically, they are workers, apprentices, trainees, engineers and technicians, managerial personnel, janitors, and security and fire personnel.

(2) Nonindustrial productive personnel: This consists of
  (a) political workers, party cadres and union officers, whose salaries are paid by the enterprise in concern; and
  (b) other operational personnel who do not directly participate in or serve the process of industrial production, including construction workers, workers in the subsidiary units engaging in nonindustrial activities, cultural workers, sanitary and medical personnel, and personnel in other attached welfare organizations.

The first category of personnel is further divided into "productive workers" and "managerial and technical personnel." It may be argued that the number of "productive workers" should be used as the basis in computing inter-industry weights. The distribution of productive workers can serve as a better indicator of the relative importance of various industries than any other employment figure, because the number of productive workers has a closer relationship to the quantity of physical output.[24] The proportions of "managerial and technical personnel" and "nonindustrial productive personnel" to total employment vary greatly from industry to industry and from year to year. Sometimes, enterprises might be able to cut the size of their "managerial personnel" or "nonindustrial productive personnel" by as much as 60% without affecting their normal production at all.[25] This fact, which is by no means unusual, seems to mean that some of these employees in Communist China have actually been part of disguised unemployment with zero or even negative marginal productivity. The Communist economists have

35

been fully aware of this situation and that is exactly why statistical authorities in Mainland China have insisted on using the number of productive workers, instead of total employment, as the denominator to compute the official figures for labor productivity.[26]

According to the provisions prevailing in 1956[27]—the year that most of the labor statistics adopted in this study were first made public—several categories of people are excluded from employment figures, though they might have contributed to industrial production at one time or another.

First of all, the so-called "number of workers and employees" appearing in official reports does not include individual handicraftsmen nor handicrafts workers in any form of cooperatives.[28] It does, however, include workers and employees in factories which use handicraft methods of production. The reasoning here is that the former are self-employed rather than paid workers, and thus their incomes are not wage incomes. The exclusion of handicraftsmen from official employment statistics creates a special problem for our treatment of handicraft production in the output indexes. A detailed discussion in this connection is postponed to a later part of this chapter.

Second, prisoners working in any production establishment are excluded from total employment figures, but their output is invariably included in the total output value.[29] This may not be a serious distorting factor in our indexes because, although forced labor has been frequently reported to exist in road-building and water conservation projects, it is of negligible importance in industrial production.

Third, it has been reported that in the period from January to November 1958 the Chinese armed forces, who participated in the construction of mines, metallurgical plants, in ore mining and the production of pig iron, steel, and rolled metal, numbered between "40 to 50 million people."[30] Another dispatch revealed that the People's Liberation Army had devoted more than 46,000,000 working-days to production in various fields in 1960.[31] According to their official statistical practice productive labor coming from the armed forces is not included in the labor statistics.[32] Since no similar information has been found for 1952, which is our weighting year, the extent to which our wage-bill weights are distorted by this factor alone cannot be determined. Presumably the participation of the armed forces in production was not very considerable until the drive of the "great leap forward" in 1958.

The defense industry in Communist China is included as part of machinery production under the Second Ministry of the Machinery Industry. It is impossible to separate employment figures for the defense industry from those of the entire machinery industry.[33]

The sources of data clearly indicate that employment figures for various industries cover enterprises in both the public and private sectors. Therefore, they are to be understood as comprising the distribution of industrial productive workers for the whole economy (of course, excluding handicraftsmen).

Employment figures are published under two designations, namely, total actual employment, whatever it covers, at the end of the year, and the annual average number of workers and/or other employees. Logically, the latter should be taken in computing our wage-bill weights. However, on some occasions, the sources of data do not indicate which figure is being used, consequently there is no way to identify the nature of the figures presented. Should these figures represent year-end numbers, there would be an overstatement in the wage-bill weights assigned to these industries because the year-end number of workers must be greater than the average number of workers in a year in which an industry is growing.

Among the thirteen industries covered in our indexes, official numbers of productive workers in 1952 are explicitly given for only five industries. For the rest of the industries, employment figures are estimated from electric power consumption per productive worker and total electric power consumption in 1952 for some industries; from the figures for average productivity and for total output values in 1952 for certain other industries; and from other information. (Detailed explanations for employment figures estimates are presented in Table C-7 in Appendix C.) In each case of estimation, attempts have been made to check the reliability of the estimates obtained.

For example, for nine industries, employment figures can be estimated from the statistics covering per-worker power consumption and total power consumption. Out of these nine industries, four have official employment figures. Therefore a comparison of the estimated figures and official figures for these four industries serves as a good check on the general reliability of the estimates for the other five industries whose official employment figures are not known. The closeness between the estimates and the known actual employment figures, as shown in Table 9, suggests that all figures estimated in this way are at least consistent with the known official figures.

Another component of our wage-bill weights is the average wage rate in each industry. A distinction corresponding to that between productive and nonproductive personnel has been made by SSB between the average wage rate of productive workers and that of total workers and other employees. Since we have decided to take the number of productive workers as our computational

TABLE 9
COMPARISON OF ESTIMATED AND ACTUAL NUMBERS OF PRODUCTIVE
WORKERS IN SELECTED INDUSTRIES

Industry	1952		1956	
	Estimated Figure	Actual Figure	Estimated Figure	Actual Figure
Coal	318,190	318,000	408,320	404,000
Petroleum	13,250		22,980	
Ferrous Metal	126,490	134,415	204,560	209,153
Metal Processing	509,980		743,820	
Chemical	72,550		117,530	
Building Materials	275,830		381,790	
Textile	777,510	777,528	941,710	942,006
Paper	53,810	53,808	56,870	56,941
Food	468,410		550,660	

Source:
See the sources of Table C-7 in Appendix C.

base, it follows that the average wage rate of productive workers should be used. However, inadequate data make it impossible to maintain this consistently throughout. Occasionally we are compelled to use average wage rates for all employees as an approximation to the desired wage rate figures. The actual difference between the two, as shown in those cases where both wage rates are known, is so small that no serious error arises in this connection.

All wage rates are on an annual basis. The official wage rate is computed in the following way:

$$\text{The average annual wage rate} = \frac{\text{the total wage fund for productive workers in the year}}{\text{the average number of productive workers}}$$

The total wage fund of an enterprise in a period is defined to comprise the following elements:[34]

The Construction of New Indexes

1. Time-rate wages
2. Piece-rate wages
3. Bonuses
4. Allowances for night work
5. Technical allowances and other special allowances
6. Allowances for high temperature and hazardous working conditions
7. Occupational allowances
8. Special allowances for instructing trainees
9. Time-off pay for nursing mothers
10. Payments for those who are absent on official duties
11. Regional allowances
12. Pay during time of transfer to employment in another locality
13. Payments to workers in training, who are still assigned to their original enterprises
14. Other allowances
15. Severance payments
16. Overtime payments
17. Additional pay for workers temporarily transferred to jobs that pay wages below the average rates of their permanent assignments
18. Wages paid to workers during work stoppages which are not due to the fault of the workers

Some items included in the wage fund, such as items (9), (12), (15) and (18), are rather unrelated to the net contribution of labor to production, and should be accordingly excluded for our purposes from a perfectionist point of view. But in practice it is impossible to single them out. We can hope that these items combined constitute only an insignificant portion of the total wage fund or that this portion may be roughly the same in all industries so that the relative importance of various industries as represented by their wage bills is not distorted. As a matter of fact, items (1) and (2), which make up the "standard wage," constitute about 80% of the total wage fund.[35]

It should be noted that although virtually all wages in 1952 were actually computed and paid in so-called "commodity-equivalent units," which represented a certain amount of composite commodities and whose monetary value varied from district to district and fluctuated over time, the official wage rate figures for 1952 were stated in money terms when published.[36] How individual wage payments in terms of "commodity-equivalent units" were converted into money terms and aggregated thereafter is not clear. Again the official data are incomplete in this connection and we have had to rely on estimates based on available information for a few industries.

C. PRICES

While more detailed explanations of, and comments on, price data and their sources will be presented in Table C-9 in Appendix C, a few general remarks are in order. Our price data come from a variety of sources. Most prices of consumer goods are those of Shanghai and Tientsin as of January 1, 1952, as quoted in the local newspapers of these two cities. They are wholesale prices, either quoted by the state trading companies or prevailing on the market. National average prices, though much preferable, are not readily available and cannot be computed since price data are so inadequate. Our chosen regional prices, however, are justifiable as intra-industry weights for consumer goods on the grounds that Shanghai and Tientsin are the two largest markets for consumer goods, and that a large proportion of the plants producing consumer goods are located in these two cities.

As to producer goods, most prices have been obtained from a price handbook compiled and published monthly by the then Ministry of Heavy Industry of the Central Government. The prices quoted in this handbook are monthly average prices; and the prices chosen for our computations are taken from the January issue of 1952. Although each issue of this handbook gives both f.o.b. factory prices and market wholesale prices, only the former are used in this study because factory price quotations greatly outnumber those for market prices, and it is desirable to have all prices on the same basis for any individual industry. Moreover, we have made use of f.o.b. factory prices for both private enterprises and state enterprises either because some producer goods were produced exclusively by private firms or because the prices of certain items only appeared in the price list for the private sector. A comparison between the prices quoted for private enterprises and those of state enterprises for identical articles shows that in most cases they did not differ significantly.[37]

Prices quoted in this issue of the handbook or in newspapers were originally in terms of the old currency. They have been converted, for our computation, into the new currency unit, which is equivalent to 10,000 old yuan, in order to make our computational work easier.

In a few cases price data are obtained from other sources, such as the directories of commodity fairs or exhibitions, or certain cost analyses given for some products. These prices usually are not for January 1952, and we have had to convert them into 1952 prices by deflating them with the official price indexes for appropriate commodity groups.

Some difficulties in dealing with the price data and the intra-industry weights calculated from this data arise from the fact that designations of most product series are so broad that each "product" actually embraces a great number of similar commodities which differ in quality, makes, and specifications.[38] On the other hand any price quoted in the newspapers or the handbook is that for a commodity of a particular specification or brand. The trouble is one of finding a representative price for a "product" so broadly designated. We have adopted a method to deal with this problem. We first calculate the range of variation of prices for each product series. If the range of variation is quite small, the unweighted average price is taken as the representative price for the product series in concern. If the range of price variation is too large, some weighting procedure, usually using quantities of the commodities of different specifications as weights, is used to arrive at a representative price.

For the purpose of illustration, let us take the prices of steel ingots to exemplify the weighting procedure. If we take all kinds of steel ingots, there are 118 prices for ingots of different specifications, ranging from a low of 380 yuan per ton to a high of 3,000 yuan per ton. An unweighted average price would not be very meaningful in this case. It is necessary, therefore, to divide the category "steel ingots" into "ordinary steel ingots" and "quality steel ingots" according to their official definitions. After this breakdown, the number of prices and their range of variation for each subgroup become as follows:

Ordinary steel ingots

Highest price	680 yuan
Lowest price	380 yuan
Unweighted average price	550 yuan
Number of prices	33

Quality steel ingots

Highest price	3,000 yuan
Lowest price	725 yuan
Unweighted average price	1,176 yuan
Number of prices	85

While the range of price variation for ordinary steel ingots has become reasonably small, it is still very large for quality steel ingots. However, quality steel ingots produced in 1952 constituted only 10.6% of the total tonnage of steel ingots produced in that year.[39] No serious error could be introduced if we weight the two average prices of the two subgroups by their relative quantities in 1952 to get a representative price for steel ingots as a whole.[40] The weighted average price then becomes 656 yuan per ton, which is much lower than the unweighted average price of 1,001 yuan per ton.

More troublesome is the determination of representative prices for the products of the machinery industry. In some instances, such as power machinery, and electric motors and transformers, the average price per set does not mean much because these products vary greatly in size or capacity. It has been found that the imputed prices per unit of capacity, such as horsepower in the case of power machinery and KVA in the case of transformers, may serve as more satisfactory indicators due to the fact that the price per set is highly correlated with capacity in these cases.

The greatest difficulty occurs in the case of metal cutting machines. This category of products is extremely heterogeneous, embracing all types of metal lathes of different sizes, degrees of precision, speeds, etc. Seventy-four prices are quoted in the price handbook. The only measure that may serve as a rough common denominator for them seems to be weight, i.e. the tonnage of metal lathes. Unfortunately, the official figures for metal cutting machines are given in terms of set numbers, except for 1952, 1953 and 1954 for which both the total number of sets and total tonnage are available. The best we can do for the time being in dealing with this item is to calculate the average tonnage per set of metal cutting machines on the basis of the known figures for 1952, 1953 and 1954, and apply it to the whole period to convert the output series into a series in terms of tonnage. Then we use the average value per ton as the unit price for this item.[41]

Needless to say this very unsatisfactory way of weighting this item is subject to a great margin of error. On the other hand, however, exclusion of metal cutting machines from the coverage of our index would have given considerable overstatement to the output index because it is the only major item among machinery products that has increased at a much slower rate than the general rate of growth of industrial production in Communist China.[42]

2. The Output Series

A. SCOPE AND CLASSIFICATION

Before output series are actually collected and weights applied, a decision must be made as to the scope that the new indexes aim to cover. The following considerations are relevant: (1) Since one of the purposes of this study is to compare the resulting indexes with the official index the scope of the new indexes must be as close as possible to that of the official index. (2) The output series or substitute indicators which can be obtained also influences our coverage. (3) The scope of these new indexes has to be determined on the basis of the available information with which we can construct weights to be assigned to all industries covered.

In general, the scope of industrial production as adopted in the construction of the new indexes is almost the same as that defined by the State Statistical Bureau of Communist China and differs from the definition recommended by the U.N. in several respects. It includes mining, manufacturing, timber production, and electric power.[43] It excludes construction.

The industrial sector as defined in this study does not include aquatic products. Aquatic production, including, according to the official definition, mainly sea and fresh-water fish catches, crustacean catches, other seafood, and fresh-water fish-breeding enterprises,[44] may be more properly regarded as agricultural or fishing activities rather than industrial production. Our definition of the industrial sector is, therefore, identical to that employed by SSB before 1958 but differing from that since 1958 in the exclusion of aquatic products.

Our new indexes should be understood to cover the defense industry, though no item of that industry is presented in the collection of output series. The production of the defense industry is treated as a missing product series, whose effect on the resulting indexes will be studied later. This decision is made on the following grounds: First, employment in the defense industry is already included in that of the metal processing industry and cannot be taken out. Second, the defense industry has occasionally produced some civilian goods which are reflected in our output series.[45]

According to the official definition, industrial activities cover repair work in various fields, but the labor spent on repair operations in all industries cannot be identified. Conceptually, the new indexes are supposed to reflect repair activities as well as manufacturing activities.

Readers may recall that the employment figures used in this study include neither individual handicraftsmen nor those in co-operatives. In view of the need for conceptual consistency and other practical obstacles we also exclude their production from our main series of indexes. In other words, this series of indexes is essentially intended to measure changes in factory production only. However, a second series of indexes inclusive of handicraft production will be made on a less satisfactory basis. The complete omission of handicraft production in the construction of an industrial output index is permissible according to the standard procedure of index making recommended by the U.N., and many countries have in fact done so.[46] Furthermore, an index exclusive of handicraft output as officially defined in Communist China may more properly measure the net results of their industrialization efforts. Handicraft production was not subject to the direct control of the Communist planning authorities. Presumably, its rate of growth would heavily reflect the results of factors other than economic planning. Due to the uniqueness and the extreme complexity of this issue, a separate section at the end of this chapter will be devoted to a more detailed discussion regarding the nature of this problem and the proposed treatment.

Having defined the general scope to be covered by this output index, we may now proceed to examine the problem of classification of industry. The Chinese Communists have classified their industrial activities according to the existing industrial ministries in the central government, such as the Ministry of Petroleum Industry, the Ministry of Food Industry, the Ministry of Textile Industry, etc. This classification not only differs seriously from the international standard industrial classification recommended by the U.N., but also changes whenever the industrial ministries are reorganized. Changes in the number of industrial ministries and their names occur almost every year (Appendix B will show the history of evolution of all industrial ministries in the regime from 1949 to

1959). Since most of the labor statistics employed in this study were released after 1956 according to the industrial classification of 1956, we must group the output series on the same basis so that the coverages of various industries will coincide with the inter-industry weights assigned to them. The individual industries are the following:

Electric industry
Coal industry
Petroleum industry
Ferrous metal industry
Nonferrous metal industry
Metal processing industry
Chemical industry
Building materials industry
Timber industry
Textile industry
Paper industry
Food industry
Daily-use commodities industry

Several things should be noted in regard to this classification. First, the metal processing industry in 1956 embraced four industrial ministries, namely the First Ministry of Machinery Industry, the Second Ministry of Machinery Industry which was the defense industry, the Third Ministry of Machinery Industry which was removed in late 1956 but reestablished in 1957, and the shortlived Ministry of Electrical Machinery Industry established in 1956 but merged into the First Ministry of Machinery Industry in 1957. Secondly, paper was controlled by the Bureau of Paper Industry, subordinate to the Ministry of Light Industry. Since employment and wage rate data are available for paper production, we have listed it as a separate industry. Thirdly, as used by the Communist economic authorities, "light industry" has been narrowly defined to include only those fields of production which do not belong to other industries on this list. It is sometimes called the "daily-use commodities industry" in Chinese Communist publications. In order to avoid any possible misunderstanding here we use this latter term.

All this has not yet solved the problem of classification to be used in constructing the over-all index. It remains to be clarified how the individual commodities are to be grouped into various industries. Often one finds that official practice has assigned certain

45

articles to different industries in different periods of time or that an item belongs to more than one industry in the same period, depending on who the actual producers are. Following are some examples of this difficulty.

Before sometime in 1957, bicycles, sewing machines, clocks, watches, radio sets, medical equipment, typewriters and electric fans were products of the machinery industry, but most of them came to belong to the daily-use commodities industry sometime after this.[47] Automobile tires had belonged to "daily-use commodities industry" prior to 1955, but became thereafter a product of the chemical industry.[48] Again, the exact date when this reclassification was made is not known. However other rubber products have remained under the jurisdiction of "daily-use commodities industry" throughout. Coke production is another confusing case. All metallurgical coke is produced by metallurgical enterprises and its value is accordingly included in their gross value of production, whereas other coke is the product of the chemical industry or the coal industry.[49] It is also interesting to note that soap is included, according to the official classification, in the food industry instead of the "daily-use commodities" industry, and manganese is regarded as a product of the ferrous instead of the nonferrous metallurgical industry.[50]

In order to achieve consistency between the coverages of the wage bills and the scopes of individual industries to which the wage-bill weights are to be assigned, we must group the output series into various industries according to the official classification prevailing in 1956. That is the classification with which the labor statistics adopted here were classified.

B. RAW DATA

Our new indexes are constructed on a foundation of output series in quantum units collected from a great variety of sources including official reports and communiques, newspapers, various issues of economic and technical journals, and other nonofficial writings quoting official production figures which cannot be obtained anywhere else. One will often find contradictions in the published figures. In most instances, however, a further investigation will reveal that these contradictions arise from one of the following sources: (1) differences in designations and coverages, such as "clocks" vs. "clocks and watches," or more commonly, figures inclusive vs. exclusive of handicraft production, (2) differences between estimated figures and actual figures, (3) differences between actual figures published in an early period and revised figures used in a later period, and (4) other computational errors, such as quantity figures derived from percentage figures, and digital errors.

The principle adopted in this study in dealing with contradictory figures due to causes other than designation differences and computational errors is that the figures published at later dates are preferred to those published earlier, and the figures given by more responsible persons are preferred to those given by less authoritative sources.

Altogether about 120 individual output series, complete and incomplete, are collected and presented as raw data, along with their sources, in Table C-1 in Appendix C. They are appropriately grouped into various industries according to the principles described in the preceding section. A digital system, which differs from that recommended by the U.N., is used in arranging the data both to help interested readers identify the classification and for easy reference. The 1-digit class is the individual industry to which an inter-industry weight is to be applied, while two or more digits denote the commodity group or the individual commodity within the industry and to which an intra-industry weight is to be applied. For any industry consisting of only one output series, no intra-industry weight is needed. A wage-bill weight is directly assigned to this commodity letting it stand for all products of that industry.

The only exception is the nonferrous metal industry. It is a very interesting fact that both Soviet Russia and Communist China have had a general policy of withholding all physical production figures for nonferrous metals. One suspects that the basic reason behind this may be that nonferrous metal production is closely associated with the production of the defense industry. However, the percentage of the total gross value of industrial production represented by the nonferrous metal industry was revealed for certain years, and the rates of growth of this industry in gross value of production terms are known for some other years. We have used this kind of information to obtain an incomplete series for the nonferrous metal industry as a whole in terms of gross value. Of course, this series, as shown in Table C-2 in Appendix C, is inferior to ordinary output series; to use it as a substitute for the latter represents our desperate attempt to remedy the data deficiency in this field.

Moreover, one will notice that even some output series pre-

47

sented in Table C-1 in Appendix C are incomplete in that production figures are missing for a number of years. Whenever the gap is small, say for only one year, it is filled by simple interpolation, i.e., by taking the arithmetic mean of the preceding and succeeding years. But, if the gap is quite long or open-ended, no such attempt is made. We simply treat these as partially omitted series, assuming that the production of the omitted items had a movement more or less similar to that of the whole industry in question in the years for which the figures are missing.

The procedures of combining complete series and incomplete series in the computation of the index are those described in the last paragraph on p. 48 in Hodgman's *Soviet Industrial Production, 1928-51*. However, in order to know to what extent the resulting index might have been affected by this treatment of missing data, we have computed the total weights of the included output data for each industry in various years. They are given in Table 10. Taking the textile industry as an illustrative example, with the total weights in 1952 as 100, the weights of known textile output data in 1953 add only to 93.52. This means that 6.48% (in terms of their intra-industry weights) of the commodities included in the base-year have no output data available for 1953. Only eight industries are listed in Table 10, each of the remaining industries is represented by a single complete commodity series and does not require intra-industry weighting.

A few items must be excluded, although they do appear in Table C-1 in Appendix C, before actual computation starts, for any of the following reasons: (1) Any commodity whose production is not known for the base year (1952) must be dropped because we cannot calculate the weight to be applied to its quantity relatives even if its 1952 price is known. That is to say, we cannot calculate $p_{52}q_{52}$ for this commodity when q_{52} is not given. It naturally follows that all new products whose production began after 1952 have to be omitted. (2) Any commodity for which the physical quantity of production is known in only one year must be excluded because it requires at least two figures to yield a rate of increase or a quantity relative.

Following is a table (Table 11) showing the number of commodities remaining in each industry after all necessary adjustments are made. The 74 commodities are those appearing in Table C-9, plus electricity, coal, crude petroleum and timber.

48

TABLE 10

TOTAL WEIGHTS OF INCLUDED OUTPUT DATA IN INDIVIDUAL INDUSTRIES IN VARIOUS YEARS

(PERCENT)

	Ferrous Metals	Metal Processing	Chemicals	Building Materials	Textiles	Paper	Food	Daily-Use Commodities
1949	96.50	88.77	96.25	100.00	93.52	75.50	80.51	61.00
1950	100.00	88.77	96.25	100.00	93.52	75.50	80.51	61.00
1951	100.00	88.77	99.75	100.00	93.52	75.50	80.51	61.00
1952	100.00	100.00	100.00	100.00	100.00	100.00	100.00	100.00
1953	100.00	99.98	99.75	99.73	93.52	100.00	97.32	93.90
1954	100.00	99.98	99.75	99.73	93.52	100.00	97.32	96.90
1955	100.00	96.25	99.75	99.73	93.52	100.00	97.32	96.90
1956	100.00	96.25	100.00	99.73	93.52	100.00	100.00	96.90
1957	98.30	84.75	100.00	100.00	99.27	100.00	100.00	100.00
1958	94.80	84.74	100.00	100.00	92.79	75.50	82.27	88.00
1959	51.30	46.14	59.80	76.23	87.54	75.50	62.06	27.00

Sources:
Computed from Table C-1 and Table C-9.

TABLE 11

NUMBER OF OUTPUT SERIES CONTAINED IN EACH INDUSTRY

Industry	Number of commodity series
1. Electricity	1
2. Coal	1
3. Petroleum	1
4. Ferrous metals	5
5. Nonferrous metals	0
6. Metal processing	18
7. Chemicals	8
8. Building materials	3
9. Timber	1
10. Textiles	14
11. Paper	3
12. Food	9
13. Daily-use commodities	10
All industry	74

Sources:
See Tables C-1 and C-9.

C. RELIABILITY OF THE OUTPUT DATA

In evaluating our new indexes of industrial production for Communist China, we must know the general reliability of the basic data with which those indexes are constructed. That is to say, we must examine very carefully the validity of the official physical output figures used in this study.

It has been openly stated by statistical authorities in Communist China that in general their industrial statistics are superior to agricultural and domestic trade statistics[51] because of the nature of industrial commodities and the relatively small number of industrial establishments. This statement, though it may be true, does not, however, inspire confidence in their industrial output data. In a country such as Communist China, industrial output statistics are liable to deliberate falsification and other types of incorrect reporting of production. It will be shown that the quality of industrial output statistics varies for different periods of time as well as for different groups of commodities. For clarity, we shall deal separately with (1) possible sources of distortions at the enterprise level, and (2) possible sources of distortions at a higher level where the aggregate output figures are processed for publication.

There are two major sources of distortion to which output figures periodically submitted by individual industrial enterprises are liable. First, reported figures may be incorrect because of an inadequate number of statistical personnel in the industrial sector, the poor professional training of statistical workers in most individual enterprises, and, occasionally, ambiguous commodity nomenclature, specification, and units of measurement. Those distortions in the reported output data which stem from institutional and organizational conditions may be called innocent errors.

The second type of distortion of industrial output data at the lower level comes from the tendency of individual state enterprises to exaggerate production. Insofar as the managerial and operating personnel in individual industrial concerns are rewarded or punished in various ways mainly according to the reported production figures, they are motivated to exaggerate production data.

Although the existence of both types of distortion in the industrial output data reported by enterprises has been proved, the first type is more frequent, except in periods when the annual goals for industrial production have been set too high to be fulfilled by most enterprises and hence the incentive to exaggerate the output data has become overwhelmingly strong. In a survey[52] conducted by the provincial statistical office in Liao-ning on the quality of the statistical data submitted in 1954 by 232 sampled state industrial establishments in that province, 14,321 cases involving doubtful figures were disclosed. Among them were 708 serious cases. Four hundred and seventy-six cases, or about 3% of the total doubtful statistical figures, were considered to be the result of deliberate falsification by the reporting enterprises. Another official source has revealed that according to overall examinations of the quality of statistical reports, about 50% of the errors found were due to the "carelessness" of statistical workers.[53]

There are several factors which tend to deter individual enterprises from falsifying their output figures. Because accurate statistical reports of production and other related economic indicators by individual enterprises are of paramount importance to the planning authorities in a Communist country, the State Statistical Bureau in Peking has announced that those reporting fictitious or false statistical figures and materials will be severely penalized.[54] Individual cases of falsifying production statistics which have been discovered by the control offices from time to time have been criticized or penalized.[55] These punitive measures are more effective in the case of physical output data than of other economic statistics which an enterprise is required to report periodically,[56] because the former are more tangible. There is less leeway for the reporting units to play with the output data without violating the state laws, and it is relatively easy for the statistical offices at higher levels to detect the falsified output figures submitted by enterprises. This is one of the reasons why more cases of falsifying output data have been revealed than cases of falsifying other statistics.

Industrial enterprises in Communist China often take a subtler and safer way to fulfill or exceed the production targets assigned to them. Instead of exaggerating the quantity they tend to reduce the quality of the commodities produced. For most industrial commodities, the standards of quality are only loosely defined; a gradual deterioration in quality can hardly be discovered by the statistical offices at higher levels, or, if discovered, can hardly be treated as a violation of state laws.

The commodity distribution system in Communist China serves as another check on the possible falsification of output figures by industrial enterprises. The distribution of all important industrial goods is subject to the control of the state.[57] All the quantities of those commodities which can be supplied by producers and the quantities demanded by users have to be reported to the central or local distribution agencies, which formulate tables known as the "material balances" on the basis of the figures reported from both sides. Producers have either to surrender physically their finished products to the distribution agencies or ship the goods directly to the users who have made contracts with the producers according to the master plan of the state distribution system in the "purchase and contract conferences" periodically held at the local or national level.[58] Plants would usually find it difficult to meet commitments if output figures were overstated. In self-interest, the users or receiving units would check the quality as well as the quantity of the goods delivered; defective or substandard goods would be returned to the producers.[59]

It is clear, then, that at any given point of time, output statistics reported by large industrial enterprises are more reliable than those of small local concerns. Large enterprises are more likely to have well-established statistical and accounting systems with better-trained personnel. Most commodities produced by large plants are so-called "important items" subject to the state distribution system, whereas many of the products made by local small factories are considered less important and the producing concerns are allowed to sell them in the market. By the same token, quality deterioration occurs more commonly in consumer goods than producer goods, because consumers, as final users, have no checking power over the quality of the commodities they have bought.

The quality of industrial output data varies during different periods of time. In general, we may distinguish three periods since the establishment of the Chinese Communist regime, namely 1949-1952, 1953-1957, and the years since 1958.

1949-1952. Immediately after the establishment of the Communist government in Peking in October 1949, a Department of Statistics was set up under the Bureau of Planning in the Financial and Economic Commission of the Government Administrative Council. With the help of Soviet statistical personnel, uniform periodic statistical schedules were prepared and put into use for major state and state-private joint enterprises in industry and construction. Since the scope of the industrial statistical services was confined to a small sector and the statistical data collected from enterprises were incomplete, the Communist central government could not confidently publish any national figures concerning economic achievements during the early years. As a rule, all official statistics at aggregate level were in terms of percentage increases, and the absolute figures in the base years were not explicitly given. Therefore, the output statistics published during this period are unreliable or even meaningless in the strict sense.

1953-1957. The situation did not improve significantly until the establishment of the State Statistical Bureau directly subordinate to the Government Administrative Council on October 1, 1952. In view of the urgent need for reliable and comprehensive data for economic planning, the newly-formed state statistical organization was charged with the responsibility of setting up a national statistical apparatus, collecting basic statistics, standardizing methods of computation and forms of statistical reports, unifying the definitions of various terms and designations, and training statistical personnel. Although some of the objectives were not completely fulfilled, the quality of statistical work, especially in the industrial sector, noticeably improved under the State Statistical Bureau between 1953 and 1957.

From the beginning, the State Statistical Bureau stressed accuracy and completeness in coverage of the periodic statistical reports which individual enterprises were required to submit regarding their production and employment. Beginning in 1953, individual industrial enterprises were ordered and helped by the State Statistical Bureau to organize and recheck their primary records of previous years. After 1954, the government published national statistics for the first time in absolute terms; the figures also included those for early years. The quality of statistical data reported by industrial enterprises considerably improved as the statistical offices were established and gradually strengthened by individual industrial enterprises during this period. Following is an official rating of the statistical services performed in 1954 by enterprises in the machinery industry.[60]

(1) The first group of enterprises constituted 8.5% of all enterprises of the machinery industry. Included in this group were those units which already had sound statistical organizations with adequate statistical personnel of good professional training, fairly well organized primary records, punctual reports of all production and employment data and more than 80% of other statistics, an established system of checking the accuracy of figures in their reports, and prompt correction of the few errors in their reports which were discovered by the statistical offices at higher levels.

(2) The second group of enterprises constituted 73% of the enterprises in this industry. Enterprises included in this group were those in which the statistical personnel, though well trained, were considered inadequate in view of the volume of work. Primary records had been organized, all production and employment data and 70% of other statistics could be punctually submitted to superior offices, a figure-checking system had been established and the errors discovered could be promptly corrected, but certain confusions still existed in their statistical forms and the data-supply systems.

(3) The third group constituted 18.5% of the enterprises in the industry, including those concerns in which the statistical offices were only newly established and were equipped with inadequate and often only poorly trained personnel. Most primary records were in a state of confusion, only 50% of statistics other than production and employment could be punctually reported, and there was no systematic check on figures; contradictory figures were occasionally found, and prompt correction could not be made for the errors discovered.

Unless the State Statistical Bureau distorted the consolidated data at publication, aggregate figures of industrial output for the period 1953-1957 may be regarded as generally reliable. However, the same is not true for the output data of 1949-1952 published after 1954. In some producing units the primary records of production were lacking for the early years; the State Statistical Bureau was compelled to make retroactive estimates about production in those plants in order to compute overall output figures for the early years. Consequently, the absolute figures of industrial output for 1949-1952 are subject to a larger margin of error.

Since 1958. As mentioned earlier, there are two sources of data distortion at the enterprise level: imperfections in the statistical system itself, and the deep-rooted incentive for industrial enterprises to overstate their performances. There are indications that the intensity of both sources of distortion has become stronger since 1958. 1958 witnessed a drastic social change in Mainland China as a result of the sudden determination of the Communist Party to communalize the whole agricultural sector. Usually each commune formed one or several "commune factories" engaging in industrial activities of one type or another. This situation was worsened by the mushrooming of small factories and workshops in urban areas all over the country under the "walking with two legs" policy, which means that both small-sized factories with indigenous methods of production and large modern factories should be developed simultaneously in every field of industrial production. So far as industrial output data are concerned, these institutional changes have had very unfortunate effects. The reliability of the output figures reported by the commune industries and native small plants is below that of previously established industrial enterprises. Most of the commune factories and the new native plants in urban areas are very small[61] and their workers work on only a part-time basis during the off-season of agricultural production.[62] Practically no one in these tiny factories has adequate knowledge of accounting and statistics. In addition, most commune factories produce only articles to be used by the communes themselves[63] so that they often do not keep any production records for the purpose of reporting.[64] Secondly, figures reported by commune and native factories are not comparable with those reported by large factories since the products are not comparable, despite identical designations. Before 1958, except for a few items, the industrial output data did not include the products of handicraftsmen. The distinction between factory production and handicraft production, however, has disappeared since 1958[65] as virtually all handicraftsmen lost their means of production as well as their independence and were "socialized" into various commune factories or local urban factories. Many Communist economists and responsible officials are fully aware of the fact that the inferior quality of the products made by commune and native plants and the inaccurate output figures reported by them have made consolidated industrial output data unreliable or unusable as economic indicators.[66]

Beginning in 1958 political pressure was also increased for individual enterprises, large and small, under the "Great Leap Forward" movement. The incentive to falsify production data became sufficiently powerful to outweigh the risks of reporting fictitious figures. It was necessary for at least some enterprises to overreport their production in order to meet the unrealistically high targets assigned to them. Once an enterprise has overreported its production by a large amount, it must continue to do so, though perhaps to a smaller extent, in ensuing years, lest the drop in production in the subsequent year would disclose the falsity of the figure reported in the first year.

Now let us examine the possible sources of distortions at the State Statistical Bureau. The fact that the central planning and statistical authorities need accurate and truthful reports from industrial units about their production is one thing, but whether the State Statistical Bureau has actually published those aggregate output figures based on the statistical reports submitted by individual concerns is quite another. Although any falsification of data at the enterprise level is regarded as a crime and the falsifier should be subject to disciplinary measures, the falsification of statistics at the high level is perfectly justified for political propaganda. It is, therefore, not inconceivable that the economic authorities in Mainland China, besides possible computational errors, might have a double bookkeeping system with one set of data for the purposes of internal planning and administration and another set for publication. Moreover, this possible source of statistical distortions could be, quantitatively, more serious than other distortions. Errors in the statistical reports due to poor clerical and computational work can be in both directions, i.e., the figures may be either higher or lower than they should have been. To a certain extent some of these errors may offset each other in the process of aggregation. As mentioned above, deliberately overreporting in the enterprise level also has its limitations.[67] However, there exist no such limitations should SSB intend to falsify aggregate output data. For this reason, the general usability of Communist China's industrial output data largely depends on whether we can convincingly prove or disprove that the Communist authorities have been operating with two sets of data.

The dramatic revision of the 1958 economic achievements announced in early 1959[68] and the tendency of SSB to withhold statistics showing a poor performance have been taken by some Western economists[69] as an indication that there is only one set of national statistics. This line of argument, while reasonable in itself, lacks rigor. In the rest of this section a number of empirical tests will be conducted for certain official industrial output data in order to determine whether they are simply figures invented by the SSB. The nature and the logic of our tests will be described below.

First, from the official statistics we have selected some technical coefficients in industrial production for various years. The selection criteria are: (1) the coefficient must be directly or indirectly related to physical output figures for the item in concern; (2) the coefficient is known to have varied within only a small range in other countries or in theory. Based on these coefficients and other available data we have made estimates of output for the items in concern for various years. We then compare the estimated output figures with official output data respectively to see the discrepancies of the two sets of figures. This is what is usually called the consistency test. However, the difficulty of the consistency test lies in the fact that while inconsistency among statistical series may be regarded as evidence of data falsification, the absence of inconsistency does not necessarily prove the contrary. Consistency among different statistical series might be attained if all data were simultaneously and systematically falsified. In order to make the results more conclusive, we must examine the values of the selected coefficients as officially published.

Since each of the selected technical coefficients is closely related to output, the exaggeration in the latter would inevitably or very likely be associated with an abnormal value for the former if the two series of official data have been simultaneously and consistently falsified. There are two possible ways of testing the validity of the official data for these technical coefficients. First, for a given technical coefficient a comparison may be made between the national average published by SSB and the average calculated from the known figures of individual plants. Fortunately, various industrial ministries have occasionally published figures of some important coefficients achieved by individual plants for the purpose of "inter-plant contest." On each occasion they usually publicize one or two "advanced" figures accomplished by certain plant or plants, and make known in the meantime figures of other individual plants which are considered less "advanced" or "backward." The purpose is to stimulate the less "advanced" or "backward" plants to catch up with what has been achieved by "advanced" plants. Judging from the motive and the circumstances under which those figures are disclosed there is little doubt that the plant figures are the actual figures reported by individual enterprises. A sample of plant figures like this is, of course, not a random sample, but, nevertheless, it sheds some light on whether the official national average is beyond the realm of plausibility. Secondly, since the technical coefficients we have selected and utilized are usually subject to only a small range of variation, their validity may be tested with international comparisons.

To sum up, the consistency test is only the starting step of the whole testing procedure. If the official data were consistent with each other simply because they were systematically falsified, the technical coefficients we have selected in carrying out the consistency test would very likely have shown abnormal values when compared with international data and/or plant data. To put it in another way, the whole testing procedure conducted here is a combination of the internal consistency test and what may be called the external consistency test.

Altogether 29 tests have been conducted here. They are presented in three groups. The first group, consisting of Tests 1-11, is comparisons of estimated output and official output for the selected industrial products, i.e., the consistency tests. Except in Test 3, we have utilized the official national averages of certain technical coefficients as our basis of estimation. Both the raw data and the computational procedures of deriving output estimates are given in Table C-6 in Appendix C. In each test we compare the estimated output with the official output to see the discrepancy between the two in quantitative terms and as a percentage of the official output figure. The results are presented in Table 12. Since most of the tests cover a number of years, we also calculate in each case the average discrepancy, that is, the average of discrepancies as percentages of official outputs in various years. They are as follows:

	Average discrepancy (%)
Test 1	2.02
Test 2	8.63
Test 3	1.47
Test 4	9.95
Test 5	2.08 (for one year)
Test 6	8.57
Test 7	3.30
Test 8	5.69
Test 9	6.09
Test 10	18.65
Test 11	8.03

In 4 tests the average discrepancies between estimated outputs and official outputs are less than 3.5%. Six tests have average discrepancies ranging from 5% to 10%. Only one test (Test 10) gives an average discrepancy as high as 18.65%. Some factors which have definitely caused estimation errors can be identified but it is hard to make any adjustment for them. One factor common to several cases is that since virtually all official figures of production capacities are year-end figures, we have to use the average of two year-end capacities as the approximate annual average capacity whenever production capacities are involved in estimating output. If the rate of capacity growth for the industry in question is constant (that is, a straight growth line in a semi-logarithm graph) or if the rate of growth has been increasing, the interpolated annual average capacity would have an upward bias. This would also be true if the construction enterprises tend to rush in the installation and construction works toward the end of the year. As can be seen in Table 12, in all the tests (Tests 1, 4, 5, 10 and 11) involving production capacities in the computations, discrepancies uniformly have plus signs (except for 1956 in Test 1), that is, the estimated output figures are larger than the official output figures.

Another common factor which has caused biases in a number of cases is that in the technical coefficients the numerators or the denominators are stated in standard units while other raw data used in estimating output, as well as the official output figures, are in natural units. In Test 4, the utilization coefficient of blast furnaces is officially defined as[70]

TABLE 12
COMPARISONS OF ESTIMATED OUTPUT AND OFFICIAL OUTPUT OF SELECTED PRODUCTS

	Unit	1949	1950	1951	1952	1953	1954	1955	1956	1957
Test 1: Use utilization hours of generating capacity to estimate output of electricity										
Estimated output of electricity	million Kwh	4,310	4,552	5,775	7,258	9,491	11,207	12,614	15,242	19,774
Official output of electricity	million Kwh	4,310	4,550	5,750	7,260	9,200	11,000	12,280	16,590	19,340
Discrepancy	million Kwh	0	+2	+25	−2	+291	+207	+334	−1,348	+434
Discrepancy as % of official output	%	0.00	0.00	0.05	0.00	3.16	1.88	2.72	8.13	2.24
Test 2: Use coal consumption rates to estimate output of thermal electricity										
Estimated output of thermal electricity	million Kwh					6,770	7,597	9,561	12,616	
Official output of thermal electricity	million Kwh					7,660	8,820	9,920	13,130	
Discrepancy	million Kwh					−890	−1,223	−359	−514	

	Units						
Discrepancy as % of official output	%		13.14	13.86	3.61	3.91	
Test 3: Estimate total output of steel by adding up outputs from different production processes							
Estimated total steel output	1000 tons	1,387				4,465	5,436
Official output of steel	1000 tons	1,349				4,465	5,350
Discrepancy	1000 tons	+38				0	+86
Discrepancy as % of official output	%	2.81				0.00	1.61
Test 4: Use utilization coefficients of blast furnaces to estimate output of pig iron							
Estimated output of pig iron	1000 tons		2,435	3,387	4,033	5,253	
Official output of pig iron	1000 tons		2,175	3,034	3,794	4,777	
Discrepancy	1000 tons		+260	+353	+239	+476	
Discrepancy as % of official output	%		11.95	11.63	6.29	9.96	

TABLE 12 (*continued*)

	Unit	1949	1950	1951	1952	1953	1954	1955	1956	1957
Test 5:										
Use utilization coefficients of open-hearth furnaces to estimate steel produced by open-hearth furnaces										
Estimated output of open-hearth steel	1000 tons								3,277	
Official output of open-hearth steel	1000 tons								3,210	
Discrepancy	1000 tons								+67	
Discrepancy as % of official output	%								2.08	
Test 6:										
Use coke ratios to estimate output of metallurgical coke										
Estimated output of metallurgical coke	1000 tons				1,790				3,878	4,706
Official output of metallurgical coke	1000 tons				2,000				4,243	5,040
Discrepancy	1000 tons				−210				−365	−334
Discrepancy as % of official output	%				10.50				8.60	6.62

62

Test 7:
Use electricity consumption in the coal industry to estimate output of coal

	Units							
Estimated output of coal	1000 tons			61,194			97,540	111,670
Official output of coal	1000 tons			66,490			98,300	110,360
Discrepancy	1000 tons			−5,296			−760	+1,310
Discrepancy as % of official output	%			7.96			0.77	1.18

Test 8:
Use the average consumption of cotton per bale of yarn to estimate yarn output

	Units							
Estimated output of cotton yarn	1000 bales	2,082	2,528	3,722	4,329	4,088	4,009	5,246
Official output of cotton yarn	1000 bales	2,410	2,680	3,620	4,100	4,600	3,970	5,250
Discrepancy	1000 bales	−328	−152	+102	+229	−512	+39	−4
Discrepancy as % of official output	%	13.60	5.70	2.80	5.60	11.10	1.00	0.08

TABLE 12 (continued)

	Unit	1949	1950	1951	1952	1953	1954	1955	1956	1957
Test 9: Use the average consumption of yarns per unit of cotton cloth to estimate output of cotton cloth										
Estimated output of cotton cloth	million meters				3,893	4,505	4,987	4,385	5,760	
Official output of cotton cloth	million meters				4,158	5,002	5,541	4,510	5,844	
Discrepancy	million meters				−265	−497	−554	−125	−84	
Discrepancy as % of official output	%				6.37	9.93	9.99	2.77	1.43	
Test 10: Use output per spindle-hour to estimate output of cotton yarns										
Estimated output of cotton yarns	1000 bales		2,776	3,315	4,143	4,914	5,561	4,903	6,440	5,069
Official output of cotton yarns	1000 bales		2,410	2,680	3,620	4,100	4,600	3,970	5,250	4,650
Discrepancy	1000 bales		+366	+635	+523	+814	+961	+933	+1,190	+419

Discrepancy as % of official output	%	15.18	23.69	14.44	19.85	20.89	23.50	22.66	9.01

Test 11:

Use output per loom-hour to estimate power loom output of cotton cloth

Estimated output of cotton cloth produced by power looms	million meters				4,066	4,378	3,699	4,911	
Official output of cotton cloth produced by power looms	million meters				3,606	4,098	3,490	4,607	
Discrepancy	million meters				+460	+280	+209	+304	
Discrepancy as % of official output	%				12.75	6.83	5.98	6.59	

Sources:

All estimated output figures are from Table C-6, in Appendix C.
All official output data are from Table C-1, in Appendix C, except the following:
  Thermal electricity, from CH, p. 64.
  Open-hearth steel, from Table C-6, in Appendix C.
  Power loom output of cotton cloth, from CH, pp. 177 and 193.

$$\frac{\text{Total converted output of pig iron}}{\text{total effective volume} \times \text{statutory work-days (24 hours each)}}$$

Similarly, output per spindle-hour (Test 10) is stated in terms of 20 count yarns[71] and output per loom-hour (Test 11) in terms of "standard people's cloth."[72] In the three cases just mentioned, there is no way to make any adjustment because of the absence of information.

Only in one instance some adjustment has been made, based partly on certain available data and partly on some arbitrary assumptions, in regard to the conversion of natural units into the standard unit. In Test 2, the coal consumption rate in thermal electric plants refers to standard coal with a heat value of 7,000 Kcal per kg[73] while total coal consumptions of thermal electric plants in various years are in the ordinary unit. However, the source which gives total coal consumptions of thermal electric plants also provides a breakdown of high-grade coal and low-grade coal.[74] In one official publication, it is said that one kg of low-grade coal is on the average equivalent to 0.7 kg of standard coal.[75] This information permits us to convert low-grade coal into standard coal. As to high-grade coal, it is officially defined as having a heat value ranging from 5500 to 8800 Kcal per kg;[76] we have arbitrarily assumed that its average heat value is 7,000 Kcal per kg. On this basis, we have converted total coal consumptions of thermal electric plants into standard units in Test 2.[77]

In addition to the two common bias-causing factors mentioned above, there are several special factors which may count for a part of the discrepancies in individual cases. In estimating pig iron output in Test 4, we have used the number of calendar days (365 days) instead of statutory work days for all years because the latter is not known. The difference between the two is the time for "major and medium repairs."[78] This may count for part of the overestimated pig iron output.[79] The same problem also arises in the case of calculating open-hearth steel output (Test 5).[80]

In Test 6 we have used coke ratios to estimate output of metallurgical coke and the estimates fall short of the official figures by 8.57% on the average. The coke ratio is higher for casting-iron than for iron to be used in steel mills.[81] Since no breakdown is given for these two types of iron in any year, we have treated all pig iron as that for making steel. Consequently, there is a downward bias in the estimated coke output. Furthermore, the numerator of the coke ratio defined by SSB is dry coke,[82] hence, our estimated coke output, strictly speaking, is dry coke too; it must be smaller in quantity than the official output of coke which does contain some moisture.

In estimating cotton yarn output in Test 8, we have made two assumptions: (1) We know the proportion of domestically produced cotton that was used to manufacture yarn in 1955. This proportion is applied to all other years for which no such information is given. But we have assumed that imported cotton would be used exclusively for the purpose of manufacturing yarn. (2) We have also assumed that the domestic production of cotton in the preceding year would be used in the current year, i.e. one year lag, but imported cotton would be presently consumed. The one year time-lag between domestic cotton production and yarn production is a reasonable assumption judging from the harvest period of cotton in China[83] and from the fact that the same assumption has been made by SSB.[84] However, to assume a constant percentage of cotton to be used for yarn spinning in various years is rather arbitrary. One alternative is to postulate that the quantity of cotton used for purposes other than yarn spinning (such as for beddings and quilted winter clothing) is a function of population. In other words, one may first calculate per capita cotton consumption for bedding and clothing needs in 1955, and use the same figure to compute the total quantities of cotton used for these needs in other years. The alternative computation has resulted an average discrepancy of 17.7% for Test 8.

The large average discrepancy in Test 10 is believed due to the fact that the actual average count number of cotton yarn produced in Communist China is higher than 20's. Two Communist sources seem to imply that the actual average count number of yarn produced has been in the neighborhood of 22's-23's.[85] If we convert our estimated output from 20's into 23's, the average discrepancy between the estimated figures and the official output data would be reduced almost to zero.[86]

To this group of tests, one more should be added as Test 12 in which we estimate pig iron output for 1959. It is singled out because it calls for more explanation than others in regard to the computational procedures. Since 1958 a great number of small-sized blast furnaces have been built; they are drastically different from ordinary (large) blast furnaces in productivity. According to *KYTCH* (p. 486), in September 1959 the total effective volume of small blast furnaces was 43,000 M³ and that of large blast furnaces was 24,000 M³. With no other information available, let us take these two figures as the annual average capacities of the two types of blast furnaces in 1959. The same source also mentions that the average utilization coefficient of small blast furnaces was 0.5 ton/m³ day in the beginning of 1959 but rose to 0.825 in September. Let us, then, assume that the average coefficient for small blast furnaces in 1959 was 0.65. Since the average utilization coefficient of large blast furnaces in 1959 is not known, we take 1958's figure (1.49)[87] by assuming that the utilization level of large blast furnaces remained roughly the same in those two years. The estimated output of pig iron in 1959 is then

$$(43,000 \times 0.65 + 24,000 \times 1.49) \times 365 = 23,254,000 \text{ tons}$$

where 365 is the number of calendar days in a year. It exceeds the official output figure (20,522,000 tons) for that year by 2,732,000 tons or 13.31%.

In summary, with due allowances given to all the identified errors in estimation, estimated output figures and the official data are certainly close enough. There is no sign that the official output data are inconsistent with other statistic series in industrial production.

In the second group of tests (Tests 13-24 in Table 13), we have compared the official national averages of the selected technical coefficients with the arithmetic means and medians calculated from data of individual plants. The number of plants or enterprises included in each sample varies. Test 23 and Test 24 are two exceptions in which we have made use of regional figures instead of plant data to calculate two average coefficients for the textile industry. There is no evidence that the official national averages of the selected technical coefficients are significantly different[88] from the averages and medians calculated from regional or plant data. More important is the fact that most of the official national averages are not better than the calculated averages and medians.

The third group of tests, as presented in Table 14, consists of international comparisons of 5 technical coefficients. Most countries included in the comparisons are Western European countries. Ideally, we should have chosen for this purpose countries with industrialization levels more or less comparable to that in Communist China, but this can hardly be done in practice because of

TABLE 13

COMPARISONS OF THE NATIONAL AVERAGES AND THE DATA FROM PLANT SAMPLES FOR SELECTED TECHNICAL COEFFICIENTS

	Period in which the sample was taken	Number of plants in the sample	Arithmetic mean	Median	Official national average
Test 13: Consumption of standard coal in thermal electric plants	1958	23	.440 kg/kwh	.465 kg/kwh	.594 kg/kwh (for 1956)
Test 14: Utilization coefficient of open-hearth furnaces	1957	15, modern	7.58 tons/m²·day	7.54 tons/m²·day	7.21 tons/m²·day
Test 15: Utilization coefficient of open-hearth furnaces	1959	12, modern	10.04 tons/m²·day	10.30–10.34 tons/m²·day	7.78 tons/m²·day (for 1958)
Test 16: Utilization coefficient of open-hearth furnaces	March 1960	12, modern	9.75 tons/m²·day	9.42–9.62 tons/m²·day	7.78 tons/m²·day (for 1958)

Sources:
Test 13: For plant data, from *Tien Li Chien She* (Power Construction). No. 12, 1958, p. 52. For the national average, from *CH*, p. 69.
Test 14: For plant data, from *YCP*, No. 4, 1958, p. 12. For the national average, from *TGY*, p. 108.
Test 15: For plant data, from *YCP*, No. 7, 1960, pp. 38–39. For the national average, from *TGY*, p. 108.
Test 16: For plant data, from *YCP*, No. 189, 1960, pp. 14–15.

TABLE 13 (*continued*)

	Period in which the sample was taken	Number of plants in the sample	Arithmetic mean	Median	Official national average
Test 17: Utilization coefficient of blast furnaces	1957	15, modern	1.205 tons/m³·day	1.235 tons/m³·day	1.333 tons/m³·day
Test 18: Utilization coefficient of blast furnaces	1959	14, modern	1.668 tons/m³·day	1.524–1.545 tons/m³·day	1.49 tons/m³·day (for 1958)
Test 19: Utilization coefficient of blast furnaces	March 1960	13, modern	1.494 tons/m³·day	1.378 tons/m³·day	1.49 tons/m³·day (for 1958)
Test 20: Coke ratio of blast furnaces	1957	9, modern	884 kg/ton	898 kg/ton	779 kg/ton
Test 21: Coke ratio of blast furnaces	1959	13, modern	841 kg/ton	702 kg/ton	711 kg/ton (for 1958)

Sources: (*continued*)

Test 17: For plant data, from *YCP*, No. 4, 1958, p. 10 and No. 7, 1958, p. 42.
For the national average, from *YCP*, No. 1, 1958, p. 8.

Test 18: For plant data, from *YCP*, No. 7, 1960, pp. 38-39.
For the national average, from *TGY*, p. 108.

Test 19: For plant data, from *YCP*, No. 189, 1960, pp. 14-15.

Test 20: For plant data, from *YCP*, No. 4, 1958, p. 10.
For the national average, from *YCP*, No. 1, 1958, p. 8.

Test 21: For plant data, from *YCP*, No. 7, 1960, pp. 38-39.
For the national average, from *Kung Fei Kung Nung Yeh Ta Yao Chin Chih Fen Hsi*, Taipei, p. 280.

TABLE 13 (*continued*)

	Period in which the sample was taken	Number of plants in the sample	Arithmetic mean	Median	Official national average
Test 22: Coke ratio of blast furnaces	March 1960	13, modern	834 kg/ton	733 kg/ton	711 kg/ton (for 1958)
Test 23: Cotton consumption per bale of cotton yarn	1956	7, regional figures	195.0 kg/bale	194.9 kg/bale	194.83 kg/bale
Test 24: Consumption of yarns per 1000 meters of cloth	1956	7, regional figures	.741 bale/1000 meters	.731 bale/1000 meters	.742 bale/1000 meters

Sources: (*continued*)
    Test 22: For plant data, from *YCP*, No. 189, 1960, pp. 14-15.
    Test 23: For regional data, from *CH*, p. 189.
             For the national average, from *CH*, p. 170.
    Test 24: For regional data, from *CH*, p. 190.
             For the national average, from *CH*, p. 170.

TABLE 14

INTERNATIONAL COMPARISONS OF SOME TECHNICAL COEFFICIENTS

	Test 25 Coal consumption in thermal electric plants (1954) (kg/kwh)	Test 26 Utilization hours of electric generating capacities (1958) (hours)	Test 27 Coke ratio of blast furnaces (1955) (kg/ton)	Test 28 Output of cotton yarns per 1000 spindle-hours* (kg)	Test 29 Cotton consumption per bale of yarn (1952) (kg)
Belgium	.507	3,860	883		159.74
Luxembourg		4,792	1,101		
France	.572	3,568	1,019	32.28 (for 1950)†	176.03
West Germany	.536	4,167	946	40.39 (for 1950)†	
Saar	.622	4,937	1,011		
Italy	.873	3,308	783		188.29
Netherlands	.490	3,138	991		206.10
Austria	.592	3,610	750	32.31 (for 1952)	175.74
Denmark	.497	2,383			
Norway	.686	4,958			205.78
Portugal	.637	2,429			
Sweden	.604	3,861	619		
Switzerland		3,389			190.32
United Kingdom	.520	3,508	982		209.32
Greece		4,247			184.70
Iceland		4,150			
Turkey	.560	2,246			
Spain		2,786	1,153		
Ireland	.752	2,828			

72

U.S.A.	.450			210.13
Japan		4,519	38.17 (for 1952)	211.00 (for 1953)
India			29.45 (for 1951)	
Hong Kong	.639	4,760 (for 1956)	41.74 (for 1953)	
Communist China		882	22.49 (for 1952)	198.97

Notes:

* The original data are in terms of British count numbers; they have been converted into 20 metric count.
† The French and German figures are the best plant performances in these two countries in 1950. The lowest output rates are 14.53 and 21.29 respectively. Other figures in Test 28 are national averages.

Sources:

Test 25: For all countries except U.S.A. and Communist China, from OEEC, *The Electricity Supply Industry in Europe*, 1956, Paris, pp. 124, 125, and 132. They refer to public utility thermal plants only. Original data have been converted into coal of a heat value of 7,000 Kcal per kg, according to the calorific value table given in *op. cit.*, p. 132 for various countries.
  For U.S.A. from *Annual Report* of the Federal Power Commission, 1955, p. 9.
  For Communist China, from *CH*, p. 77.

Test 26: For all other countries, from OEEC, *The Electricity Supply Industry in Europe*, 1960, Paris, pp. 39 and 54.
  For Communist China, from *CH*, p. 68.

Test 27: For Communist China, from *TCKI*, No. 18, 1957, p. 33. It is the arithmetic mean of the coke ratio for casting iron and the coke ratio for pig iron to be used in steel mills.
  For all other countries, from J. F. Deuhurst and others, *Europe's Need and Resources*, 1961, New York, p. 1131.

Test 28: For France and West Germany, from *Productivity Measurement*, Vol. II, OEEC, 1956, Paris, p. 118.
  For Austria, from *Productivity Measurement Review*, No. 9, May 1957, p. 6.
  For Japan, from K. Seki, *The Cotton Industry of Japan*, 1956, Tokyo, p. 171.
  For India, From S. D. Mehta, *The Indian Cotton Textile Industry: An Economic Analysis*, 1953, Bombay, p. 12.
  For Hong Kong, from A. S. Pearse, *Japan's Cotton Industry*, 1955, England, p. 122.
  For Communist China, from *CH*, p. 170.

Test 29: For Japan, from K. Seki, *op. cit.*, p. 91.
  For Communist China, from *CH*, p. 170.
  For all other countries, from OEEC, *The Textile Industry in Europe*, 1957, Table 27, and 1956, p. 90.

the lack of this type of statistical information in backward countries. Nor have we made use of similar data of other Communist countries simply because it is logically implausible to compare Communist China's data with data the reliabilities of which remain to be established. In Test 25, coal consumed in thermal electric plants in various countries has been converted into what is called by the Chinese Communists standard coal with a heat value of 7,000 Kcal per kg.[89] As can be seen, the coal consumption rate in thermal electric plants in Communist China is higher than that in 12 countries among the 15 noncommunist countries compared. In Test 29, cotton consumption per bale of yarn in Communist China is higher than that in 6 countries but lower than that in 5 countries. The disparity of cotton consumption in spinning is due to different kinds of cotton used and the variation of the average count number of yarns produced. The cotton consumption rate remains approximately constant for low and medium count yarns but it rises slightly for yarns over 60 count.[90] Difficulties arise in making an international comparison of yarn output per spindle-hour owing to the fact that the production rate varies greatly as the count number of yarn changes. Output rates referring to yarns of specific count numbers have been obtained for only 6 countries including Hong Kong. All these output rates have been converted into 20's yarn in Test 28. This international comparison is inconclusive and uncertain because of the unidentified yarn count system in Communist China. A change in the measurement of yarn count took place in Communist China in this period. Up to 1957 the British system was used to measure the yarn count.[91] In 1958 SSB was in the process of changing the British system into the metric system and both systems were used in that year.[92] Only since 1959 the metric system has become the standard measurement of yarn count.[93] Since all the textile data of Communist China are taken from publications of 1958 or later years and there is no indication as to the basis of the yarn count numbers, we do not know whether the output rate per spindle-hour for Communist China refers to 20 British count or 20 metric count.

The use of dry coke in computing coke ratios of blast furnaces in Communist China is again reflected in her relatively low figure in Test 27. There are, of course, other factors affecting the coke ratios in various countries, such as the quality of iron ore.

In the international comparison of utilization hours of electric generating capacities, as shown in Test 26, Communist China is higher than 17 countries but lower than only 3 countries. However, this finding is fairly reasonable rather than surprising. Power plants in Communist China usually have no sufficient reserve capacities to meet the peak-load demand in the year. Restricting power consumption of some less important users or sectors during peak-load periods has been a common practice.[94] It is quite natural that the utilization period of the existing power generating capacities in Communist China appears to be longer than that in those countries in which electric plants always keep enough reserve capacities to meet the peak-load demands. The longer utilization period of power plants in that regime is also attributed to her peculiar pattern of power consumption. As a rule, the difference between the peak-load and the off-peak load is smaller in industrial uses than for lighting and residential uses. On the average, more than 80% of power generated in Communist China is consumed by the industrial sector,[95] while this proportion is much lower in other countries.[96] The more even load curve in Communist China permits the Chinese power plants to operate with smaller reserve capacities. As a matter of fact, of the three countries having utilization periods longer than that in Communist China, Luxembourg and Saar are also the only two among those compared here in which the proportion of industrial power consumption is higher than that of the Chinese.[97] Norway has a long utilization period because the very low tariff of Norwegian power has provided an incentive to develop industries calling for very long period of use, such as electro-chemistry and electro-metallurgy.[98]

As a conclusion, in the tests conducted above, there is no evidence that the aggregate output data published by the Communist statistical authorities are invented figures. In the tests in group I, the closeness of the estimated output series and the official output data means that the official output data are in general consistent with other economic statistics. Tests in group II and group III, on the other hand, have not revealed any indication that the technical coefficients from which we have derived our estimates are abnormally high or low. The tests in group I, which by themselves merely establish the internal consistency among various official statistic series but not necessarily the reliability of those series, have become reliability checks after the technical coefficients are compared with international data and plant data.

D. ADJUSTMENT FOR HANDICRAFT PRODUCTION

A few peculiar facts existing in the official data covering handicraft production create a unique problem and call for special treatment in constructing these new indexes. The term "handicraft production" may be used in a broad sense or in a narrow one. In the broad sense, handicraft production comprises the following four elements:

(1) Handicrafts attached to agriculture. This category consists of handicraft production by farmers or their family members, usually during off-seasons. These handicraft goods may or may not go into the market for sale. Gross value of output in this sector in 1952 was estimated to be 6.7 billion yuan.[99]

(2) The production of individual handicraftsmen and artisans and their assistants. These people have already lost their status as primary producers in agriculture and they invariably earn their incomes by selling their products in the market.

(3) The production of handicraftsmen in cooperatives of various forms. Although their production activities are carried out in a collective manner, each individual maintains his status as an independent operator. The combined gross value of output of both category (2) and category (3) in 1952 was reported to be 7.3 billion yuan.[100]

(4) The production of the factories employing handicraft methods. These factories are called handicraft factories and differ from so-called "modern factories" in that they are not equipped with machinery and mechanical power. However, workers in handicraft factories receive their incomes in the form of wages.

In official statistical practice, production in category (1) is classified as by-products of agriculture and its value is included in figures for agricultural production. As to category (4), its production is combined with that of modern factories under the general title of "factory production" in computing both output and labor statistics. Only categories (2) and (3) are enumerated as "handicraft production" in all official statistical reports,[101] and we try to follow the official usage of the term in the narrow sense.

The crucial point which concerns us is not the question whether the official classification and definitions are conceptually acceptable but the problem of making the coverage of the index consistent for all years. This becomes a serious problem because of the following two facts.

(1) The output quantities released by the Chinese Communists for the years before 1958 are not uniform in excluding or including handicraft production. Among the 74 output series to be used in computing the new indexes, 10 items contain handicraft production for the years before 1958.[102] They are the following:

Coal
Pig iron
Timber
Cotton cloth
Colored and printed cloth
Silk fabrics
Paper
Sugar
Salt
Edible vegetable oil

(2) To make things even worse, in 1958 virtually all handicraftsmen, both individuals and those in cooperatives, were socialized and brought into either state factories or factories of the people's communes, though there had been some slowly paced, gradual socialization before 1958. Accordingly, all output data, except for those items which cannot be produced by handicraft methods, in 1958 and thereafter included output turned out by former handicraftsmen.

To deal with these complications, we must try either to have all output series include handicraft output or to eliminate handicraft production from all series for all years. The difficulties of estimating handicraft output for each of the more than 60 series in which the official figures for the years before 1958 exclude handicraft production are inconquerable and make the first of the two theoretical alternatives unavailable. In addition, to include handicraft production would make the coverage of the output series not comparable with that of the wage-bill weights because employment figures used in this study do not include handicraftsmen in various fields. What we can do with reasonable accuracy is to subtract from the above listed 10 series actual or estimated handicraft production for each year before 1958.

We then have 74 output series which are uniformly exclusive of handicraft production for 1949-1957, but in which all handicraft production is inextricably included for 1958 and 1959. Based on these output series, a series of index numbers are made; let us call them "unadjusted index numbers." We then multiply the unadjusted index numbers of 1958 and 1959, respectively, by a ratio of the total gross value of industrial production of the current year minus the gross value of handicraft production of 1957 to the total gross value of industrial production of the current year. To illustrate, we may write the ratio for 1958 as follows.

$$\frac{\text{Total gross value of 1958} - \text{handicraft production of 1957}}{\text{Total gross value of 1958}}$$

The implicit assumption involved here is that the production by former handicraftsmen in 1958 and 1959 would remain the same as in 1957, in terms of gross output value, and the difference between the total gross value of output of 1958 or 1959 and handicraft production in 1957 would represent the achievement made by those factory workers who were not newly transferred from the handicraft sector.

The resulting output index after this adjustment is made should thus be interpreted as one that measures what would have been the changes in industrial production of factories exclusively, had there been no such drastic socialization of handicraft production. This index may reasonably serve as an indicator reflecting the net results of the industrialization of Communist China in the period studied.

It is also desirable to know the effect of handicraft production on the changes of total industrial output in that country. But this can be done only in a very rough manner. Based on the actual and estimated figures of handicraft output for the ten commodities listed in Table C-4,[103] we construct an output index for handicraft production in the period 1949-1957. 1952 prices are used here as weights. Since the quality of handicrafts-produced pig iron, cotton cloth, print cloth, silk fabrics, paper, sugar and salt is inferior to that produced in factories, we have chosen the lowest prices quoted for those commodities instead of the averaged prices given in Table C-9. As to crude coal, timber and edible vegetable oil, whose quality is believed independent of the methods of production, we have decided to use the average prices as weights.

To obtain an output index for both factories and handicrafts we combine the factory production index and the handicraft production index with the net output values of the two sectors in 1952 as weights. Their net output values are derived in the following way.

78

According to Ma Yen-chu, the ratio of net value to gross value of factory production in 1953 was 0.3253.[104] Assuming that this ratio in 1952 was the same as in 1953, net value of factory production in 1952 should then be 8,790 million yuan.[105] On the other hand, total net value of industrial output inclusive of handicraft production in 1952 is given as 10,931 million yuan.[106] Therefore, net value of handicraft output in 1952 is

10,931 — 8,790 = 2,141 million yuan.

8,790 and 2,141 are the two figures used as weights in combining the two indexes.

CHAPTER V

Evaluation and Implications of the New Indexes

1. Evaluation

The new indexes constructed in this study are intended to remove or minimize some of the biases in the official indexes measuring industrial growth in Communist China during the period of 1949-1959. It is, however, impossible to remove all potential biases. Moreover, some new biases and errors undoubtedly have been created in the new indexes due to the use of a hybrid weighting system, and the inadequate, sometimes even unreliable, official output data, labor statistics and price data. Unfortunately, in most instances we know neither the magnitude nor the direction of the possible errors and biases. For example, it is desirable to use several sets of weights taken from different periods in order to test the weight effects mentioned in Chapter II; but we could not do this simply because statistical information is insufficient to make a second set of weights from another time period. What will be done in this section is: (1) to evaluate the new indexes on the basis of the output coverage; (2) to determine the extent to which the new indexes are biased because of the omission of certain groups of commodities; and (3) to point out other biases in the new indexes, for which we know the directions but not the magnitudes.

One important way to evaluate the general reliability of an output index is to examine the coverage of the physical output series on which it is based. The following table (Table 15) shows 1952 gross values calculated for the commodities produced by factories in different industries (as well as the total) as percentages of the gross values given by the SSB for 1952. For each industry the calculated gross value is $\Sigma p_{52}q_{52}$ for the commodities included. It should be noted, however, that since the official gross values computed from the "factory-reporting method" may differ from those which would have been obtained from the formula Σpq, these percentages serve only as rough indicators of the completeness of the coverage of the index for each industry and for the industrial sector as a whole; they do not represent the actual coverages.

TABLE 15

COMPARISON OF CALCULATED GROSS VALUES OF INDUSTRIAL OUTPUT AND OFFICIAL GROSS VALUES IN 1952

Industry	Official Gross Value (in Million Yuan)	Calculated Gross Value (in Million Yuan)	Ratio (%)
Electric Power	431	—*	100.0
Coal	830	827	99.6
Petroleum	207	30	14.5
Ferrous Metal	1,366	—	100.0
Nonferrous Metal	614	—	100.0
Metal Processing	2,732		
Machine-Building	1,401	624	44.5
Other Metal Products and Repairs	1,331	0	0
Chemical	1,123	500	44.5
Building Materials	621	283	45.6
Timber	1,216	—	100.0
Textile	8,070	7,563	93.7
Paper	697	151	21.7
Food	6,105	5,836	95.6
Daily-Use Commodities	3,002	725	24.2
All Industry	27,020	20,166†	74.6

Sources:
    For calculated gross values, from Tables C-1 and C-9 in Appendix C. Some official gross values are directly given in *CH*, p. 53. Others are computed from the percentages of the gross values of individual industries to the total industrial output value, as given in *TGY*, pp. 87, 92, and 94, and *HCKTKY*, p. 59. They may not add to the total because of rounding and/or the processes of converting percentage figures into absolute value figures.

* "—" indicates that the coverage is known to be complete and no calculated gross value needs to be presented here.
    † This is the sum of all the calculated gross values plus the official gross values for those items whose coverages are complete.

The fairly high ratio (74.6%) of calculated gross value to official gross value for all industries indicates that our new indexes have a solid base so far as coverage is concerned. The ratios for a few individual industries appear to be too low, but not all of them are very damaging. For the petroleum industry, whose ratio is only 14.5%, we have taken a single item, namely crude petroleum, to stand for all products made from crude petroleum. There is a close correlation between the output of crude petroleum and the output of its refined products, thus the rate of change in the former may serve as a good indicator of the rate of change in the latter, or the whole industry. In the case of paper production, which also has a very low ratio (21.7%), we have included only final products such as newsprint, cigarette paper and cardboard, whereas the official value figure also includes raw materials, that is, pulp. The only industries really suffering from insufficient coverage are the daily-use commodities industry and the category "other metal products and repairs."

The validity of an output index whose coverage of physical output series is not complete also depends on the nature and the behavior of the commodities omitted in the computations. Ordinarily, a general index of output with incomplete coverage is interpreted as a measure of the growth of total output because it is assumed that the production of all omitted items combined would follow the general pattern of movement shown by the output index, but indications seem to suggest that this assumption may not hold in the case of Communist China. It is necessary to analyze the nature and the behavior of the products omitted in computing our indexes. It is also desirable to determine the extent to which our indexes would be affected if this assumption did not hold here.

Products omitted in our calculations may be classified into three categories: (1) military end-products; (2) new products for which production began after 1952; and (3) other products for which output figures are not given by the Chinese Communist authorities. The nature of these three groups of products differs, hence they should be examined separately.

(1) The production of military goods is controlled, exclusively, by the Second Ministry of Machinery Industry in the central government of Communist China. Although no output figure in this field has ever been published, we have reasons to believe that the growth rate of this industry would be higher than the general rate of growth for total industrial output. In other words, the average annual rate of increase in the output of military end-products would be higher than the 23.7% registered by our index of factory production for the period 1949-1959. However, this does not necessarily mean that our index has understated the industrial growth of Communist China. Readers may recall that inter-industry weights have been applied in the process of computing the overall output index, and that the weight assigned to the metal processing indus-

try, of which the production of the Second Ministry of Machinery Industry is one of the components, is the total wage bill of that industry in 1952. Hence, as long as the growth rate for the production of military end-products did not exceed the rate of growth for the metal processing industry calculated in this study, the omission of military end-products does not cause any understatement in our overall index. The pertinent questions then are: Did the output of military end-products grow faster than the metal processing industry in general, and if so, by how much? Unfortunately, available information does not permit us to give answers to either question in exact terms.

(2) The second group of products which have not been covered in our indexes are new products for which production began only after 1952. Unlike the case of military end-products, new products did not concentrate in a single industry. Following is a table showing some incomplete statistics of the number of new products manufactured in each industry during the period 1953-1956.

TABLE 16

NUMBER OF TRIAL-MANUFACTURED PRODUCTS IN
SELECTED INDUSTRIES DURING 1953-1956

Industry	Number of Trial-Manufactured Products
Petroleum	46
Ferrous Metals	553
Nonferrous Metals	217
Metal Processing	2,783
Chemical	451
Building Materials	22
Total	4,072

Sources:
  People's Handbook, 1958, p. 450.

A few remarks are in order concerning these figures. Most of these trial-manufactured products are variants of some existing commodities, with only slight differences in specification, capacity, or design; and they have been actually counted in some of the output series used in this study. For example, all new types of steel ingots and rolled steel manufactured after 1952 have been counted in the total tonnages of steel ingots and rolled steel in the years after 1952. This is equally true in the cases of higher grade cement, metal cutting machines for new functions, and power machinery of higher capacity. After eliminating all these products, one finds that a majority of new goods, differing drastically from existing goods, which are not included in our computations, are in the metal processing and chemical industries. Another industry that may have manufactured a large number of new products since 1952 is the daily-use commodities industry.

Presumably, output of new goods would increase at a high rate precisely because they were new. Table 17 gives average annual

TABLE 17
AVERAGE ANNUAL RATE OF INCREASE OF SELECTED NEW PRODUCTS
IN THE METAL PROCESSING INDUSTRY

Commodity	(%) Average Annual Rate of Increase	
6.7 Power generating equipment	229.5	(Over 1957-1959)
6.12 Motor vehicles	211.0	(Over 1956-1958)
6.14 Tractors	485.0	(Over 1958-1959)
6.15 Combine harvesters	351.8	(Over 1955-1959)

Sources:
Calculated from the output data in Table C-1 in Appendix C.

growth rates of four new products in the metal processing industry, for which we clearly know that production began only after 1952 and for which the output figure for each year is available. Average annual rates of increase for all four items are very high—exceeding 200%. It is believed that some new products in the chemical industry must also have astonishingly high rates of increase, although we have no data to calculate them. For new products in the daily-use commodities industry, the general rate of increase would probably be much lower than that demonstrated by new goods in the metal processing and chemical industries.

Our knowledge about the behavior of the output of military end-products and new goods is so limited that we are unable to determine directly from our information the effect on our general output indexes of omitting these items. But we do know one thing: no matter what the rate of increase has been for these items, their value of output has been counted in the official figures for output value. Therefore, part of the discrepancy between the official rates of increase and the rates revealed by our indexes in the metal processing, chemical and daily-use commodities industries is attributable to the exclusion of military end-products and new products.

Table 18 compares the official average annual rates of increase for the metal processing and chemical industries with our estimates. This comparison is confined to the period 1952-1957 because rates before 1952 are less relevant and no such data are available for the years after 1957.

Now, let us arbitrarily assume that half of these discrepancies is due to the exclusion of new goods and/or military end-products in our computations and the other half is due to the combination

TABLE 18

OFFICIAL AND ESTIMATED AVERAGE ANNUAL RATES OF INCREASE IN THE
PRODUCTION OF THE METAL PROCESSING INDUSTRY AND THE
CHEMICAL INDUSTRY (1952-1957)

	Metal Processing Industry	Chemical Industry
Official Average Annual Rate of Increase	30.9%	30.7%
Estimated Average Annual Rate of Increase	22.1%	25.7%
Discrepancy	8.8%	5.0%

Sources:

The official rates are calculated from the official output values for 1952 (given in *CH*, p. 53) and 1957 (derived from the percentage distribution of gross output values in various industries in 1957, as given in *TGY*, p. 92.

The estimated rates are from Table 24. They are the average annual rates of increase for factory production.

of all other biasing factors. One will then find that omitting products and military end-products in these two industries would have an effect on the average annual rate of increase for total industrial production of no more than 0.74 percentage point.[1]

Lack of information prevents our making similar comparisons for other industries which have manufactured some new products after 1952. However, in view of the fact that new goods produced by other industries, such as the daily-use commodities industry, have had much lower rates of growth compared with new goods in the metal processing and chemical industries, it is safe to say that the omission of new goods other than new machinery and new chemicals could not significantly affect the average annual rate of increase for the whole industrial sector as calculated in this study. It could not be affected, let us say, more than 0.26 percentage point. This amounts to saying that, in all likelihood, the omission of all new goods and military end-products could have caused at most an understatement of one percentage point in the average annual rate of increase for factory production as a whole as determined by our index.

(3) Now we must proceed to examine the last category of omitted items, i.e., all those civilian goods for which output figures have not been revealed by the Chinese Communist authorities. These items constitute the bulk of total omitted products. More specifically, the gross value of all items in this category combined, as of 1952, represents more than 17.5% of the total gross value of factory production in that year,[2] or about 70% of the total gross value of all omitted items.[3]

It is a well-known fact that the Communists, in China as well as in other Communist countries, are very selective in publishing their production statistics. They have a strong tendency to publish those output figures most favorable to their propaganda but withhold those figures which are less favorable or harmful from a political point of view. In other words, the output series we are able to obtain are very likely to be those having relatively high rates of growth. By the same token, at least some of the civilian products absent from our output series compilation are exactly those whose production increased at smaller rates or even declined. Production of certain goods has even terminated because of the appearance of new substitutes.[4]

Here let us make another arbitrary, but not unreasonable, assumption as to the general rate of increase for the third category of omitted items as a whole—suppose that the average annual rate of increase for those items combined was approximately equal to the lowest rate of growth among the thirteen industries in this study. The lowest rate of average annual increase occurred in the textile industry, with 13.8% and 6.5% for the periods 1949-1957 and 1952-1957 respectively. For the same periods, the average annual rates of growth as registered by our index of factory production are 20.5% and 14.4% respectively. The discrepancies are then 6.7% and 7.9%, which, if multiplied by the weight 0.18, become then 1.2 and 1.4. This means that, with our above assumption as to the rate of growth of the third category of omitted products, the average annual rate of increase in our index of factory production would have an overstatement of 1.2 or 1.4 percentage points. Either 1.2 or 1.4 is more than enough to offset the understatement of 1.0 percentage point caused by the omission of military end-products and new goods produced after 1952.

Furthermore, there are some upward-biasing factors which

Evaluation of the New Indexes

cannot be corrected in the construction of our indexes due to data deficiencies. For instance, it has been disclosed[5] that private industries tended to under-report their production figures, either to avoid or lighten the tax burden, or because of a general attitude of non-cooperation with, or hostility toward, the Communist government. The private sector in Communist China shrank gradually until 1956 when practically all private enterprises were socialized. Our indexes were biased upward in this connection simply because the under-reporting element diminished year after year until it completely vanished.

Considering all the factors discussed above, I am inclined to believe that the indexes of industrial output computed in this study still have a slight bias on the high side, although I am not able to determine the margin or magnitude of this error. Any reader who wishes to use these indexes for further economic analysis of Communist China is warned about this limitation.

Readers are also warned concerning the accuracy of index numbers since 1958. The general quality of index numbers since 1958 is inferior to that for earlier years, not only because less confidence can be placed in the underlying output data after 1958, but also because the actual number of commodities used in the computations decreases sharply after 1958.

Finally, like all production indexes, there is no way of allowing for changes in the quality of products. In most Western countries' cases this factor creates a downward bias in the production index, but the situation is not so clear in the case of Communist China. On one hand, most machinery products have been improved in quality over time. On the other hand, deterioration has been frequently revealed in Communist writings for some commodities, especially among consumers' goods. Moreover, fluctuation in quality has had a cyclical pattern. Each big production push led to quality deterioration, invariably followed by a new movement aimed at improving quality.

2. The Rate of Growth of Industrial Production

Presented in Table 19 are two new series of industrial output indexes for Communist China constructed according to the methodology discussed in previous chapters. The first series is exclusive of handicraft production while the second covers both factory and handicraft production. The second index is in general less valid than the first index because of the imperfect way of adjusting for

87

Rate and Pattern of Industrial Growth in Communist China

handicraft production. Therefore, most of the conclusions and implications regarding the economy of Mainland China are drawn on the basis of the first index.

It is quite clear from comparing the new indexes with the official indexes that the latter have greatly exaggerated the rapidity of industrial development in China. Taking 1952 = 100, the new index number for factory and handicraft production in 1959 is 330.9 whereas the official index records 528.6. This represents a 60%

TABLE 19
NEW INDEXES OF INDUSTRIAL PRODUCTION
IN COMMUNIST CHINA, 1949-1959
(1952=100)

	Production of Factories				Production of Factories and Handicraftts			
	New		Official		New		Official	
	Index	Annual Increase (%)	Index	Annual Increase (%)	Index	Annual Increase (%)	Index	Annual Increase (%)
1949	44.3	—	39.9	—	50.0	—	40.8	—
1950	57.7	30.3	52.0	30.3	63.3	26.6	55.7	36.6
1951	77.0	33.5	74.8	43.8	81.2	28.4	76.8	37.8
1952	100.0	29.8	100.0	33.7	100.0	23.1	100.0	30.2
1953	124.7	24.7	131.7	31.7	122.1	22.1	130.2	30.2
1954	141.6	13.5	153.6	16.6	139.4	14.2	151.4	16.3
1955	146.9	3.7	165.6	7.8	149.7	7.4	159.8	5.5
1956	182.2	24.0	217.1	31.1	179.4	19.8	205.0	28.3
1957	195.9	7.5	240.6	10.8	189.8	5.8	228.3	11.4
1958	272.6	39.2	—	—	251.5	32.5	379.4	66.2
1959	371.4	36.3	—	—	330.9	31.6	528.6	39.3

Sources of official indexes:
See Table 2.

overstatement (528.6/330.9 = 1.60) in the official index showing the rate of industrial growth over a period of 7 years, if our new output index is considered closer to the true picture. Only in 1955 the annual increase in output as registered by the official index fell short of that shown by our new index. The difference between the two sets of indexes widens year after year since 1949. So, if 1949 is taken as the base year, the official index number for 1959 is 195.8% of the new index number for that year. The largest discrepancy between our new index and the official index occurs in 1958, implying that the "great leap forward" claimed by the Chinese Communists for industrial output in 1958 was much lower than it appeared to be. No official index for factory production has been reported for the years since 1958 because the division of production into handicrafts and factories disappeared after the socialization of handicrafts in 1958. We are thus unable to tell the exact extent to which the official index of factory production has been exaggerated for years after 1958.

Comparison may also be made between our factory production index and the index of net value added in manufacturing factories, mining and utilities estimated by Professor T. C. Liu and Dr. K. C. Yeh for Mainland China in the period 1952-59.[6] This series has

TABLE 20
COMPARISON OF THE INDEX OF FACTORY PRODUCTION
WITH LIU-YEH ESTIMATES, 1952-59
(1952=100)

	Our Index of Factory Production	Liu-Yeh Estimates
1952	100.0	100.0
1953	124.7	122.9
1954	141.6	142.2
1955	146.9	159.0
1956	182.2	210.8
1957	195.9	238.6
1958	272.6	289.2
1959	371.4	373.5

Sources of Liu-Yeh estimates:
    T. C. Liu and K. C. Yeh assisted by C. Twanmo, *The Economy of the Chinese Mainland: National Income and Economic Development, 1933-1959*, RM-3519-PR, the RAND Corporation, April 1963, Table 8, Vol. I, p. 94. The figures cited here are the sums of the net value-added of manufacturing factories, mining, and utilities at 1952 constant yuan.

been constructed on a basis comparable in a very broad sense to that used in this study.

As is shown in Table 20, our index numbers are almost identical with those of Liu-Yeh's for 1953, 1954 and 1959; but differ for the remaining years. In general, our index shows a slightly slower rate of growth before 1958 than that suggested by Liu-Yeh's value-added figures.

However, even after the tremendous overstatement of the official indexes is removed, the rate of growth of industrial production in Communist China remains very impressive. With 1952 = 100, the new index of factory production rose to 371.4 in 1959, while the new index inclusive of handicraft production reached 330.9 in 1959.

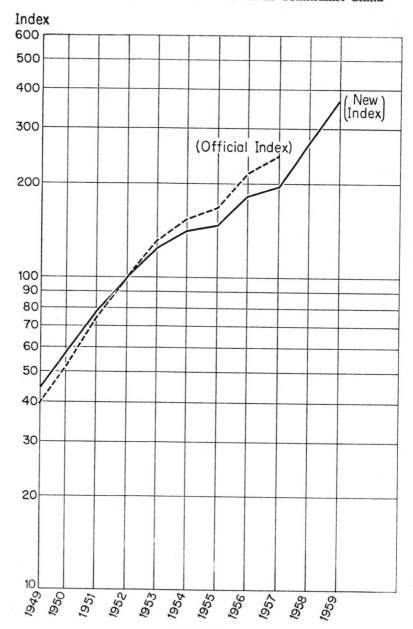

FIGURE 1
INDEX OF INDUSTRIAL PRODUCTION
BY FACTORIES, 1949-1959
(1952=100)

Index

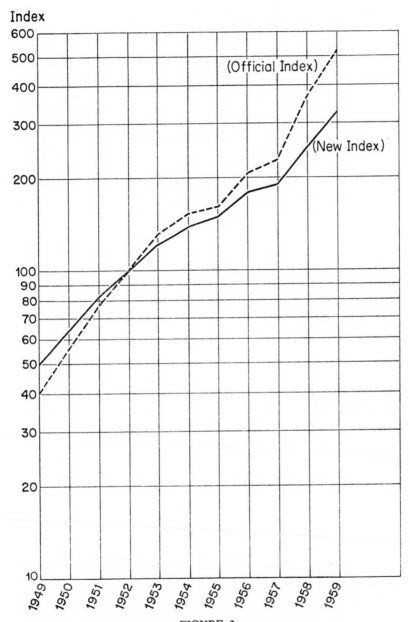

FIGURE 2
INDEX OF INDUSTRIAL PRODUCTION BY
FACTORIES AND HANDICRAFTS, 1949-1959
(1952=100)

91

Rate and Pattern of Industrial Growth in Communist China

An inspection of the year-to-year changes in our new indexes shows that the pace of economic development in Communist China was not steady. The annual rates of increase in both new series of indexes fluctuate, and the patterns of fluctuation are almost identical to those shown by the official indexes.[7] They were in general lower during the First Five Year Plan (1953-57) than in the period of economic rehabilitation (1949-52) and the first two years (1958-59) of the Second Five Year Plan. 1958 saw the highest rate of annual increase, 39.2% in factory productions, for the whole period covered by this study. The tempo of growth hit its low points in 1955 and

TABLE 21
AVERAGE ANNUAL RATE OF GROWTH OF INDUSTRIAL
PRODUCTION IN COMMUNIST CHINA
(PERCENT)

Period	Factory Production	Production of Factories & Handicrafts
1949-1957	20.5	18.1
1952-1957	14.4	13.7
1949-1958	22.4	19.7
1952-1958	18.2	16.6
1949-1959	23.7	20.8
1952-1959	20.6	18.6

Source:
Calculated from Table 19.

1957, with annual rates of increase in factory production of 3.7% and 7.5% respectively.

Accordingly, the average annual rate of industrial growth also varies, depending on the period used and whether or not handicraft production is included. For the entire period covered in this study, the average annual rate of growth of factory production is 23.7%, whereas that of production including handicrafts is 20.8% (Table 21).

Owing to rapid growth of population in Mainland China, the growth rate for industrial output per capita, as shown in Table 22, is much lower than aggregate output. However, the rate of advance in industrial output is still greater than the rate of population growth.

The preceding discussion was concerned with the increase in consolidated output figures, either inclusive or exclusive of handicrafts, and with its relationship to population growth. It is also important to examine the relative development of various individual industries which make up the whole industrial sector of the country.

Readers recall that all commodity quantities before 1958 exclude any handicraft production while the output data for years since 1958 include the production of handicrafts; and that there is no way to remove handicraft production from output figures for each commodity for the years after 1958. We therefore constructed

TABLE 22

INDEXES OF POPULATION AND INDUSTRIAL OUTPUT PER CAPITA IN
COMMUNIST CHINA, 1949-1958

(1952=100)

	Population	Factory Production	Production of Factories and Handicrafts
1949	94.3	46.9	53.0
1950	96.1	60.0	65.8
1951	98.0	78.6	82.9
1952	100.0	100.0	100.0
1953	102.2	122.0	119.4
1954	104.6	135.4	133.3
1955	106.9	137.4	140.0
1956	109.2	166.8	164.3
1957	113.0	173.3	167.9
1958	117.6	231.8	213.8
Average Annual Rate of Increase		19.6	16.8

Source:
    Population data are from the U.N. *Monthly Bulletin of Statistics*, June 1961, p.1. According to the footnote, they are official mid-year population figures or means of official year-end figures.

an unadjusted general index based on the output series without handicraft production for the years before 1958 and the output series with handicraft production for the later years. We then deflated the unadjusted general index numbers for the years since 1958 by certain ratios. The resulting index is the general index of factory production cited in this chapter. Of course, this adjustment method cannot be applied to individual industries. Therefore, to be conceptually consistent, we examine here only the output indexes of individual industries up to 1957, that is to say, indexes of factory production only.

The second thing that should be noted is that, unlike the general index which is constructed with wage bills as inter-industry weights and unit gross values as intra-industry weights, the output index for each individual industry is based purely on gross value weights.

It is apparent from Table 23 that producer goods industries have been the core of industrialization in Communist China, while industries chiefly producing consumer goods have lagged well behind so far as growth rates are concerned. Taking the period of 1952-1957 for example, the electric power, petroleum, ferrous metal, nonferrous metal, machine building and chemical industries displayed higher rates of growth, all of their average annual increases

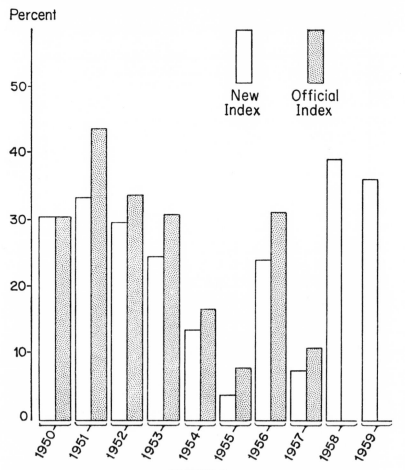

FIGURE 3
ANNUAL INCREASE OF FACTORY PRODUCTION
1949-1959

94

exceeding 20%. The lowest rates are found in the textile industry
and the food industry, with a 6.5% and 9.3% increase per annum
respectively.

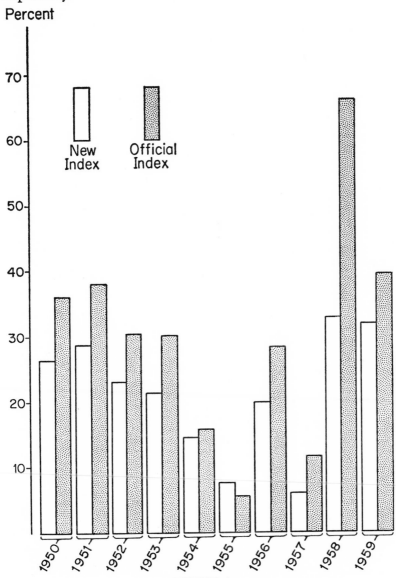

FIGURE 4
ANNUAL INCREASE OF FACTORY AND HANDICRAFT PRODUCTION
1949-1959

95

TABLE 23
OUTPUT INDEXES OF VARIOUS INDUSTRIES, 1949-1957
(1952=100)

Industry	1949	1950	1951	1952	1953	1954	1955	1956	1957
Electricity	59.4	62.7	79.2	100.0	126.7	151.5	169.1	228.5	266.4
Coal	48.8	64.7	79.9	100.0	104.8	125.1	147.3	166.7	197.7
Petroleum	27.8	45.9	70.0	100.0	142.7	181.0	221.6	266.7	334.4
Ferrous Metal	11.3	42.3	65.9	100.0	129.3	156.0	198.8	299.9	353.7
Nonferrous Metals	17.4	—	—	100.0	—	—	207.1	—	370.0
Machine Building	18.1	16.9	40.5	100.0	138.1	184.4	220.8	351.3	271.5
Chemicals	17.8	32.8	67.9	100.0	127.4	172.4	172.2	246.6	314.2
Building Materials	29.6	54.9	86.5	100.0	130.6	157.6	150.9	204.8	241.6
Timber	51.4	58.2	66.4	100.0	152.0	177.7	124.8	106.8	199.6
Textiles	48.5	65.8	77.9	100.0	117.4	129.3	113.5	150.5	136.7
Paper	29.0	37.9	64.8	100.0	140.5	164.2	162.1	194.1	220.1
Food	54.3	55.4	72.5	100.0	113.7	127.5	143.4	148.2	156.2
Daily-use commodities	57.2	70.4	95.5	100.0	133.0	131.0	142.0	151.8	174.5

Evaluation of the New Indexes

In summary, our new indexes have eliminated some of the accumulated upward biases embodied in the official indexes of industrial output and scaled down the index number by nearly one half by the end of the period covered in this study. Yet the new indexes remain a quite impressive record of industrialization. However, this industrial development is characterized by imbalance, intertemporal as well as intersectoral.

TABLE 24
AVERAGE ANNUAL RATE OF INCREASE, BY INDUSTRY
(PERCENT)

Industry	1949-1957	1952-1957
Electricity	20.6	21.6
Coal	19.1	14.6
Petroleum	36.5	27.3
Ferrous Metal	53.8	28.7
Nonferrous Metal	46.5	29.9
Machine Building	40.3	22.1
Chemical	43.1	25.7
Building Materials	30.0	19.3
Timber	18.5	14.8
Textile	13.8	6.5
Paper	28.8	17.1
Food	14.1	9.3
Daily-use Commodities	15.0	11.8

Sources:
Calculated from data in Table 23.

A further question may be asked as to the possible future rate of growth of industrial output in the regime. Indications seem to suggest that the growth rate of industry in the near future will be lower than that achieved in the past. This is to be expected because, among other things, some great advantages the Chinese Communists have enjoyed in the past should gradually disappear. For one thing, the past high rate of growth has been achieved with the aid of technical assistance and imports of modern machinery and equipment from Soviet Russia. Due to the Sino-Soviet dispute, these advantages are now diminishing; Communist China has begun to depend more heavily on her domestic supply of most producer goods and solve technical problems with her own technicians. Thus the future rate of industrial growth will depend very much on the existing capacity of industry and the supply of technicians and skilled labor.

Indications also show that the Chinese Communists have begun to place greater emphasis on agricultural production, relatively neglected in the First Five Year Plan. This would naturally reduce investment funds available to industry in the next few years.

In fact, the Chinese Communist Party, having learned from bitter experience the consequences of unbalanced development of the national economy and having suffered extreme hardship due to crop failures in 1959 and 1960, announced the new decision about economic planning for 1961 in the Ninth Plenary Session of the Eighth Central Committee:[8]

> In planning for heavy industry in 1961, the scope of capital construction should be appropriately reduced, the rate of development should be readjusted and a policy of consolidating, filling out, and raising the standards should be adopted on the basis of the victories already won.

This new policy was reconfirmed by an editorial of *JMJP*, the official organ of the Chinese Communist Party, on the occasion of the 12th anniversary of the regime.[9] The Communist government had already, said the editorial, reduced the scope of capital construction in 1960, readjusted the rate of industrial development and turned its main energy to strengthening the weak links.

It is also very interesting that in 1961 for the first time since the beginning of the regime there was a complete absence of published statistical figures or indexes whatsoever concerning the economic achievements of the preceding year and plans drafted for the current year. The complete blackout of statistical data by the government has caused a strong suspicion that the economic plan for 1960 must have turned out to be a fiasco and that output in most industrial sectors must have been seriously reduced.

3. International Comparisons

Economists are always tempted to make international comparisons of aggregate economic accounts in order to assess the economic performance of various nations, although such comparisons undoubtedly involve conceptual and statistical hazards due to large institutional differences in the nations compared and different estimating methodologies employed. The desire to make such comparisons between a Communist country and other non-Communist countries has become even keener since the world divided into two polarized camps. People are interested in knowing the relative strength, or what is called the "gap," between the two camps and the change in this relative strength over time.

Evaluation of the New Indexes

With carefully selected indicators and cautious interpretations of the results, an international comparison of this sort may be worthwhile. The incomparability of various national aggregates is believed less serious if the comparison is made in terms of relative rates of growth. We shall try in this section, therefore, to compare the growth of industrial output in Communist China, as shown in this study, with that in other countries in two different ways. First, we shall compare the rates of industrial growth in Communist China with those achieved by certain other countries, chiefly non-Communist ones, in the same period. Second, a comparison will be made of the performances displayed in the industrial sectors by selected countries in their First and Second Five Year Plans.

Table 25 presents general indexes of industrial production for the U.S., USSR, U.K., Czechoslovakia and Communist China in the period from 1951 to 1960, plus those of eight non-Communist countries which showed relatively high industrial growth rates in the past decade. For all non-Communist countries chosen here, the official indexes are adopted because they have been constructed by more or less standardized procedures as recommended by the UN.[10] The Soviet and Czechoslovakian series are from independent estimates made by Western economists on a methodological basis similar to that employed in this study.[11] Other Communist countries are not presented in this table for comparison because their production indexes are computed exclusively on the basis of gross values of production and there are no independent estimates made by non-Communist economists on a basis comparable to that used by the Western countries.

It can be seen that the rate of growth of industrial production of Communist China in the last decade has exceeded that of most non-Communist countries as well as the Soviet Union and Czechoslovakia. The only exceptions are Pakistan whose production index with 1952 = 100 is higher than that of Communist China in several years, and Japan which took the lead in 1957 by a few percent. However, Communist China grew faster than Pakistan in the years before 1952 and again in the years after 1958.

These relationships are even clearer if we compare the countries in terms of average annual rates of increase over a given period. As shown in Table 26, if the period 1952-1957 is taken, the average annual growth rate of industrial production for Communist China, which is 14.4%, is lower than Pakistan's rate of 19.7%, and slightly lower than the 15.0% rate for Japan. If the period 1952-1958 is

99

TABLE 25
INDEXES OF INDUSTRIAL PRODUCTION FOR SELECTED COUNTRIES
1951-1960
(1952=100)

Country	1951	1952	1953	1954	1955	1956	1957	1958	1959	1960
Austria	99	100	102	116	136	141	149	153	159	172
France	99	100	101	111	121	134	145	152	158	175
Western Germany*	93	100	110	123	141	152	162	166	178	198
India	97	100	102	109	118	129	133	135	147	164
Italy	97	100	110	120	132	141	151	156	174	200
Japan	93	100	120	130	140	173	201	202	251	314
Mexico	100	100	101	108	120	131	140	148	161	—
Pakistan	79	100	128	164	206	233	246	276	308	333
United Kingdom	103	100	105	112	118	119	121	119	126	135
United States	97	100	109	102	115	118	120	111	126	129
Soviet Union	94	100	114	130	138	150	158	168	n.a.	n.a.
Czechoslovakia	92	100	103	107	121	129	142	157	172	n.a.
Communist China	77	100	125	142	147	182	196	273	371	n.a.

Sources:

For Communist China, from Table 19, for the Soviet Union from N. M. Kaplan and R. H. Moorsteen Indexes of Soviet Industrial Output, RM-2495, the RAND Corporation, May 13, 1960, p. 235; for Czechoslovakia, from G. J. Staller, "Czechoslovak Industrial Growth: 1948-1959," American Economic Review, June 1962, p. 389; for all other countries from the U.N., Monthly Bulletin of Statistics, Aug. 1960, pp. 20-25 and June 1961, pp. 20-26.

* Excluding West Berlin and the Saar.

TABLE 26
AVERAGE ANNUAL RATES OF INCREASE IN INDUSTRIAL PRODUCTION FOR SELECTED COUNTRIES
(PERCENT)

Country	1951-1958	1951-1959	1951-1960	1952-1957	1952-1958
Austria	6.4	6.1	6.3	8.3	7.3
France	6.3	6.0	6.5	7.7	7.2
Western Germany	8.6	8.4	8.7	10.1	8.8
India	4.8	5.4	6.0	5.9	5.1
Italy	7.1	7.6	8.4	8.6	7.7
Japan	11.8	13.2	14.5	15.0	12.4
Mexico	5.8	6.1	n.a.	7.0	6.8
Pakistan	19.4	18.4	17.3	19.7	18.4
United Kingdom	2.1	2.5	3.0	3.9	2.9
United States	2.0	3.3	3.3	3.7	1.8
Soviet Union	8.7	n.a.	n.a.	9.6	9.0
Czechoslovakia	7.8	8.1	n.a.	7.3	7.8
Communist China	19.8	21.7	n.a.	14.4	18.2

Sources:
Computed from data in Table 25.

TABLE 27
AVERAGE ANNUAL RATES OF INDUSTRIAL GROWTH OF COMMUNIST CHINA, SOVIET RUSSIA AND INDIA DURING THEIR FIRST AND SECOND FIVE YEAR PLANS
(PERCENT)

Communist China	Soviet Russia*		India
20.6 (1952-1959)	Kaplan-Moorsteen's: (1927/28-1937)	10.4	5.4 (1951-1959)
	Nutter's (I):† (1928-1937)	11.1	
	Nutter's (II):† (1928-1937)	9.9	
	Hodgman's: (1927/28-1937)	14.2	

Notes:
* The average annual rates of growth computed from Kaplan-Moorsteen's estimates and Hodgman's estimates are averages of 10¼ years while that of Nutter's is an average of 10 years.
† Nutter's (I) is based on 1928 weights, Nutter's (II) on 1955 weights.

Sources:
For Communist China, from Table 21.
For Russia, from N. M. Kaplan and R. H. Moorsteen, *Indexes of Soviet Industrial Output*, RM-2495, The RAND Corporation, May 13, 1960, p. 226; G. Warren Nutter, "Industrial Growth in the Soviet Union," *American Economic Review*, Vol. XLVIV, May 1958, Papers and Proceedings, p. 402; and D. H. Hodgman, *Soviet Industrial Production, 1928-1951*, Harvard University Press, Cambridge, 1954, p. 237.
For India, from Table 26.

101

Rate and Pattern of Industrial Growth in Communist China

TABLE 28
COMPARISON OF OUTPUT OF MAJOR COMMODITIES IN COMMUNIST
CHINA, SOVIET RUSSIA AND INDIA DURING THEIR FIRST
AND SECOND FIVE YEAR PLANS

Commodity	Communist China (1952-1959)	Soviet Russia* (1927/28-1935)	India (1951-1958)
Electric Power Production (1,000,000 Kwh)			
At the beginning of the period	7,260	5,007	5,856
At the end of the period	41,500	26,294	12,372
Average annual rate of increase (%)	28.3	25.7	11.3
Coal Production (1,000 M.T.)			
At the beginning of the period	66,490	35,510	34,980
At the end of the period	347,800	108,900	46,068
Average annual rate of increase (%)	26.7	16.7	4.0
Steel Ingots Production (1,000 M.T.)			
At the beginning of the period	1,349	4,251	1,524
At the end of the period	13,350†	12,588	1,848
Average annual rate of increase (%)	38.7	16.1	2.8
Pig Iron Production (1,000 M.T.)			
At the beginning of the period	1,929	3,283	1,848§
At the end of the period	20,522†	12,489	2,148§
Average annual rate of increase (%)	40.2	20.2	2.2
Iron Ore Production (1,000 M.T.)			
At the beginning of the period	4,287	6,133	3,720
At the end of the period	n.a.	27,078	6,132
Average annual rate of increase (%)	28.5‖	22.7	7.4

Evaluation of the New Indexes

TABLE 28 (*continued*)

Commodity	Communist China (1952-1959)	Soviet Russia* (1927/28-1935)	India (1951-1958)
Cement			
Production (1,000 M.T.)			
At the beginning of the period	2,860	1,850	3,252
At the end of the period	12,270	4,489	6,168
Average annual rate of increase (%)	23.1	13.0	9.6
Cotton Yarn			
Production			
At the beginning of the period	3,620 (1,000 bales)	n.a.	592 (1,000 M.T.)
At the end of the period	8,250 (1,000 bales)	n.a.	764 (1,000 M.T.)
Average annual rate of increase	12.5		3.7

Sources:

For Communist China, from Table C-1 in Appendix C.

For U.S.S.R., from Hodgman, *Soviet Industrial Production 1928-1951*, Table (A)(i), pp. 194-204.

For India, from *U.N. Monthly Bulletin of Statistics*, July 1957, pp. 27-62 and June 1960, pp. 28-65.

Notes:

* Average annual rates of increase for U.S.S.R. are averages over 7¼ years.

† Excludes production by indigenous methods.

§ Includes output of pig iron and ferro-alloys.

|| Average over the period 1952-1957.

taken, the average annual rate of increase of Communist China is about the same as Pakistan's (18.3% vs. 18.4%) and higher than any other country's listed here. But, if any period covering more years than 1952-1958 is taken for comparison, Communist China has the largest average annual rate of increase in industrial production.

We may further compare the average rates of industrial growth achieved respectively by Communist China, Soviet Russia and India during their First and Second Five Year Plans. As shown in Table 27 the growth rate in Communist China during the First Five Year Plan and the first two years of the Second Five Year Plan is almost four times the Indian rate of a comparable period. The Soviet rate is about 50% to 70% of the Chinese rate, depending upon which estimate on Soviet Russia is taken for comparison. Among the four estimated Soviet rates, Hodgman's is less comparable than the other three with the Chinese rate computed in this study because the output data used by Hodgman in computing his index excludes the production of small enterprises in Soviet Russia. The other three estimates of Soviet growth agree very closely with one another. It is, therefore, more reasonable to assume that the Soviet average annual rate of industrial growth is about 50% of the Chinese rate during their First and Second Five Year Plans.

This finding is supported by a more straightforward comparison of the physical output of more or less identical products for these three countries during a period of a given length after the inauguration of the First Five Year Plan. Table 28 represents such a comparison for seven major products which, mostly producer goods, are chosen merely because they are most homogeneous and comparable among all physical output data officially published by these three countries.

It is clear that for all the items compared, Communist China achieved a higher growth rate than Soviet Russia during the first seven years of the "eras of economic planning." In the cases of steel and pig iron, Chinese output in 1952 was much lower than that of Soviet Russia in the year preceding the Soviet First Five Year Plan, but the Chinese Communists exceeded Soviet output by a sizable margin at the end of a seven year period.

When we compare Communist China and India, the difference in growth rates is even more spectacular for every commodity compared in Table 28. In one case, steel, the ratio of average annual rates of increase in output for these two countries is 18:1. Perhaps the picture would be more favorable or less unfavorable to India if some consumer goods were compared because greater emphasis was given to the production of consumer goods in India in the First and Second Five Year Plans.

Effects of Industrialization
and Production Indexes

It is a well-known fact that there is no single, unequivocal formula which will yield index numbers capable of measuring the changes in overall production perfectly. More paradoxically, while index numbers are designed to measure changes in certain factors in an economy, the fewer and smaller changes there are the more accurately index numbers can measure, and the more and greater changes there are the less meaningful index numbers become. The index number problem is, therefore, more serious for an economy undergoing rapid industrialization than for a mature economy. It is important for index makers as well as users to have a full understanding of the limitations of any production index made from a given formula for an economy in rapid industrialization.

In figure 5, MM is the production possibilities curve in period 0 for an economy which is assumed to have produced two final products, x and y only. M'M' is the new production possibilities curve of the same economy in period 1.[1] The combinations of x and y actually produced in the two periods are represented by points A and B respectively. The line NN is the market price line in period 0, tangent to MM at A. N'N' is a line parallel to NN through the point B. Similarly, TT is the market price line in period 1 and tangent to M'M' at B. T'T' is drawn through the point A parallel to TT. The fact that B is at a higher level than A but lies on the right side of OADE line indicates that outputs of both x and y have increased from period 0 to period 1, but x has increased faster than y. The numerical value of the base-weighted output index (Laspeyres') is the ratio OE/OA. Similarly, the current-weighted output index (Paasche's) is represented by the ratio OD/OA.[2] In our diagram, Laspeyres' formula yields a larger index number than Paasche's (OE/OA is greater than OD/OA), because the relative price of x, the faster growing product, has declined from period 0 to period 1, and, as a result, x is assigned a smaller weight in Paasche's formula than in Laspeyres'. This is a case of an economy which ordinarily tends to expand production of a commodity more rapidly if the marginal rate of transformation is

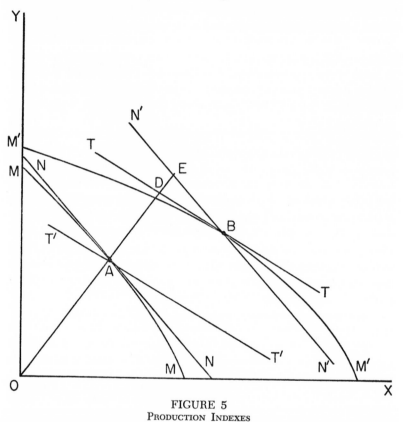

FIGURE 5
PRODUCTION INDEXES

moving in the direction in favor of this commodity. On the other hand, the relative price would change in conformity with the change in the marginal rate of transformation. Symbolically, x grows faster than y because $\triangle x/\triangle y$ at B is greater than $\triangle x/\triangle y$ at A. Since $\triangle x/\triangle y = Py/Px$ at A and B, the tangent points of the market price lines and the production possibilities curves in the two periods, Px/Py is smaller at B than at A.

This situation, however, may not necessarily occur in a planned economy where planners do not determine industrialization policy solely on economic grounds. In such an economy, development of some industries may be particularly stressed even though the marginal rate of transformation is moving against them.[3] Paasche's index number would then exceed Laspeyres'.

In the aforesaid analysis, one oversimplification, among others, is that the economy is assumed to have produced only two finished goods. Output indexes are constructed in the real world usually for a great number of products among which some are the intermediate goods or raw materials for producing other goods. In view of this complication, it is necessary to make two modifications in connection with the above interpretation of index numbers. First, instead of an individual product, x represents a group of products whose rates of growth are relatively high, i.e., exceeding the average rate of growth of all products; and y is a group of products having growth rates lower than the average rate. Secondly, in the previous discussion, market prices are identical with net values of the products. Now, since some goods are used as raw materials or intermediate goods in producing other goods, there is a divergence between the price and the value added of a commodity. The weights are then interpreted as the value-added units which we use V_x and V_y to denote. Therefore, the resulting indexes become the value-added unit weights indexes. For the convenience of further discussion, let us call Laspeyres' index, index (I) and Paasche's index, index (II).

For the reason already mentioned, (I) will be greater (smaller) than (II) if V_{1x}/V_{0x} is smaller (greater) than V_{1y}/V_{0y}.

If market prices instead of value-added units are used as weights, one obtains the gross-value weights indexes, again in the following two possible forms:

The index (III) with P_{0x} and P_{0y} as weights, and
the index (IV) with P_{1x} and P_{1y} as weights.

(III) will be smaller than (IV) if P_{1x}/P_{0x} is greater than P_{1y}/P_{0y}, and the reverse relation holds if P_{1x}/P_{0x} is smaller than P_{1y}/P_{0y}.

By definition $V = P - C$ for any commodity in a given period,[4] that is, the difference between the selling price (P) and the costs of raw material consumed per unit of product, as represented by C. Consequently, any change in the process of industrialization affecting V, P, and C would have some impact on the outcome of output index computations. Two phenomena are often observable in developing countries.

Rate and Pattern of Industrial Growth in Communist China

(a) In general, industrialization is a process of increasing the roundaboutness or intermediacy of production. In other words, the number of stages in manufacturing or fabrication of industrial goods tends to increase in the course of industrialization. In one sense this seems to mean that the general degree of double-counting in aggregate gross value tends to rise as the value of the same amount of raw materials would be repeatedly counted an increasing number of times. In another sense, it would imply that the rapidly-growing goods are very likely to be those turned out in later stages of the fabrication process so that their prices contain a larger share of value added by earlier stages of fabrication than the less fabricated goods. Specifically, this is a case where P_{0x}/P_{0y} is greater than V_{0x}/V_{0y} and P_{1x}/P_{1y} is greater than V_{1x}/V_{1y}. So (III) is greater than (I), and (IV) is greater than (II).

(b) Another situation often found in some developing countries is that when output of x is increased more rapidly than other products, its relative price tends to fall. As P_{1x}/P_{1y} is smaller than P_{0x}/P_{0y}, (IV) is smaller than (III). This observation is known as the "Gerschenkron effect".[5] The decline in relative price of the faster-growing product may be realized through, among other things, the following two different ways.

(1) Increases in production of certain commodities may have come as a result of improved technology in producing those commodities. Technological advances reduce production costs, hence permit producers to sell increased quantities at lower prices. Now let us first assume that the technological improvement has been made exclusively in the direction of saving material costs.[6] It can be the reduction of raw material waste, better utilization of scrap, the substitution for expensive materials cheaper materials which could not be used previously because of technical difficulties, more efficient use of fuel by an improved generating and transmitting system, or increased recapture of waste heat. This is a case where both Cx and Px have declined in relation to Cy and Py, but Vx/Vy may have risen. So (III) is greater than (IV) and (II) may be greater than (I).

(2) Another possibility is that the technological progress is primarily in the direction of improving labor and/or capital productivity without reducing materials consumed per unit output. Or this sort of gain is obtained from the economy of scale in production[7] when output has been considerably increased. Px declines but Cx may not fall, or may even rise because the increased

108

demand for the materials used to produce this commodity may bid up prices of the raw materials. At any rate, both Vx/Vy and Px/Py decline. So (III) is greater than (IV), and (I) is greater than (II).

If the conditions of (a) and (b-1) are met, we know (III) is greater than (I), (IV) is greater than (II), (III) is greater than (IV) and (II) is greater than (I). So an ordering can be obtained as follows

$$(III) > (IV) > (II) > (I).$$

That is, under these conditions, the numerical values of the index numbers computed from the four formulae would appear in such a descending order.

Similarly, if the conditions of (a) and (b-2) are met, we obtain that:

$$(III) > (IV) > (II) \text{ and}$$
$$(III) > (I) > (II).$$

So, among the four formulae, the output index with early year prices as weights is the largest while the index based on late year value-added units as weights is the smallest. The other two formulae would yield results somewhere in between.

Mathematically, the discussion of an output index based on wage-bill weights is analogous to that of the gross-value weights index. Instead of unit prices, one uses here unit wage costs (r) as an approximation of value-added units for all commodities. Therefore, he has to compare the relative movement of r and V for various industries.

The difficulty in understanding the weight effects of a wage-bill weights formula when applied to a developing country lies in the fact that we have meager knowledge of the relative movements of unit wage costs and value added for individual industries in the course of industrialization. The ratio of unit wage costs to value added in each product is determined essentially by the natural endowment of the economy, the capital structure and labor productivity in the industry under consideration, and workers' bargaining power and other dynamic factors in labor markets. All of these tend to change when the industrial sector moves from economic backwardness to a higher stage of development.

Table A-1 contains some information regarding this problem as compiled and processed by the Department of Economic and Social Affairs, United Nations. Data of value added per unit of wages and salaries are furnished for various manufacturing indus-

TABLE A-1
VALUE ADDED PER UNIT OF WAGES AND SALARIES IN MANUFACTURING INDUSTRIES OF SELECTED COUNTRIES

CLASS I

Industry	Australia			Canada			Denmark		New Zealand		
	1938/1939	1948/1949	1953/1954	1938	1948	1953	1948	1953	1938/1939	1947/1948	1953/1954
Food, beverages & tobacco	2.43	2.02	2.03	2.52	2.49	2.53	2.29	2.14	1.98	1.96	2.10
Textiles	1.70	1.63	1.73	1.70	1.81	1.56	2.00	1.68	1.20	1.81	1.82
Clothing, footwear & madeup textiles	1.57	1.56	1.55	1.48	1.75	1.62	1.54	1.50	1.27	1.41	1.42
Wood products & furniture	1.60	1.64	1.68	1.51	1.87	1.77	1.56	1.53	1.64	1.63	1.79
Paper & paper products	2.27	2.00	2.31	2.04	2.58	2.47	2.18	1.98	2.00	2.00	2.72
Printing & publishing	1.68	1.67	1.71	1.65	1.75	1.77	1.58	1.69	1.70	1.77	1.87
Leather & leather products	1.70	1.59	1.55	1.57	1.72	1.43	1.90	1.61	2.00	1.44	1.67
Rubber products	1.87	1.45	1.73	2.52	2.22	2.43	1.71	1.71	—	1.67	2.47
Chemicals & chemical, petroleum, & coal products	2.95	2.37	2.62	2.53	2.80	2.69	2.36	2.38	2.57	2.39	2.67
Nonmetallic mineral products	1.92	1.56	1.68	2.43	2.28	2.23	1.65	1.91	2.11	1.96	2.29
Basic metals	2.18	2.19	1.77	2.69	1.95	2.19	2.40	2.96	2.00		2.00
Metal products	1.49	1.41	1.52	1.79	1.79	1.78	1.67	1.60	1.65	1.64	1.69
Other manufacturing	1.68	1.61	1.72	1.80	1.78	1.77	1.72	1.66	4.00	2.00	1.64
All manufacturing	1.84	1.66	1.72	2.02	2.05	2.02	1.84	1.78	1.78	1.76	1.88
Mean deviation	.35	.25	.24	.40	.32	.37	.28	.31	.44	.23	.34

TABLE A-1 (continued Classes I and II)

| | Class I | | | | | | | | Class II | | |
| | Norway | | | United Kingdom | | United States | | | Argentina | | |
Industry	1938	1948	1953	1948	1954	1939	1947	1954	1939	1948	1954
Food, beverages & tobacco	4.19	6.65	4.75	2.57	2.38	2.52	2.42	2.23	1.76	2.62	3.29
Textiles	1.68	2.00	1.86	2.04	1.75	1.66	1.88	1.57	1.58	2.51	2.49
Clothing, footwear & made-up textiles	1.56	1.73	1.65	1.71	1.56	1.59	1.72	1.60	1.37	2.00	2.64
Wood products & furniture	1.36	1.57	1.26	1.67	1.52	1.63	1.78	1.63	1.60	2.16	2.52
Paper & paper products	1.71	3.29	2.36	2.11	2.26	2.00	2.25	2.07	1.58	3.03	2.93
Printing & publishing	1.59	1.69	1.62	1.88	1.68	1.81	1.87	1.73	2.11	2.10	2.72
Leather & leather products	1.57	1.70	1.75	2.38	1.65	1.67	2.13	1.60	1.65	2.29	3.03
Rubber products	2.46	2.29	2.05	1.91	1.83	1.79	1.66	1.80	1.69	3.65	3.41
Chemicals & chemical, petroleum & coal products	3.07	2.69	2.37	2.20	2.58	2.93	2.78	2.66	1.93	4.12	3.59
Non-metallic mineral products	1.33	1.58	1.80	1.76	1.74	2.07	1.90	1.97	1.65	2.12	2.61
Basic metals	2.40	2.16	2.71	1.66	1.85	1.80	1.59	1.84	1.60	2.22	2.19
Metal products	1.49	1.59	1.71	1.57	1.61	1.77	1.65	1.73	1.53	1.86	2.32
Other manufacturing	2.08	1.89	2.09	1.70	1.76	1.77	1.70	1.72	1.37	2.46	3.17
All manufacturing	2.00	2.36	2.17	1.80	1.79	1.93	1.87	1.86	1.65	2.39	2.74
Mean deviation	.62	.85	.55	.25	.25	.28	.28	.23	.14	.50	.37

TABLE A-1 (*continued Classes II and III*)

Industry	Class II Union of South Africa			Japan		Class III Mexico			Venezuela	
	1937/ 1938	1947/ 1948	1952/ 1953	1948	1953	1939	1944	1950	1936	1953
Food, beverages & tobacco	3.48	2.62	2.83	3.49	3.32	4.05	3.87	3.70	3.46	3.16
Textiles	1.74	1.78	2.08	2.73	2.65	2.00	3.26	2.22	1.67	2.23
Clothing, footwear & made-up textiles			1.73	2.27	2.21	2.14	2.50	1.95	2.00	2.34
Wood products & furniture	1.65	1.74	1.84	2.30	2.04	1.94	2.11	2.57	2.50	2.23
Paper & paper products	1.90	1.98	2.23	2.77	3.06	2.66	3.40	3.14	1.00	2.34
Printing & publishing			1.76	2.14	2.56	1.51	1.75	2.03	1.67	1.80
Leather & leather products	2.00	1.73	1.65	3.80	2.09	2.32	2.89	2.49	2.45	2.77
Rubber products	4.33	3.00	2.94	2.22	2.81	3.38	2.66	4.86	1.67	3.82
Chemicals & chemical, petroleum & coal products	3.60	2.89	2.97	2.46	3.57	2.21	4.30	3.58	3.33	3.30
Non-metallic mineral products	2.40	2.02	2.23	2.16	2.79	2.29	2.74	2.83	1.97	2.49
Basic metals	1.49	1.53	2.58	1.97	2.35	2.57	4.31		2.50	2.19
Metal products			1.55	1.72	2.06	1.14	1.38	2.86	2.38	1.95
Other manufacturing	1.60	2.65	1.85	2.16	2.01	1.86	3.54	2.12	4.12	2.62
All manufacturing	1.97	1.88	1.98	2.18	2.54	2.39	3.32		2.79	2.66
Mean deviation	.83	.48	.42	.45	.42	.52	.74	.64	.65	.44

112

TABLE A-1 (continued Class IV)

Industry	Brazil 1939	Brazil 1949	Brazil 1953 (Class IV)	India 1948	India 1953
Food, beverages & tobacco	4.88	5.56	4.25	2.72	3.45
Textiles	2.92	2.95	2.72	1.97	1.48
Clothing, footwear & made-up textiles	2.83	2.81	2.52		1.67
Wood products & furniture	2.44	3.11	2.55	3.04	1.87
Paper & paper products	3.04	3.91	3.77	2.12	2.48
Printing & publishing	2.23	2.67	2.19		1.41
Leather & leather products	3.49	3.54	3.07	1.81	1.79
Rubber products	3.82	5.36	4.41		2.80
Chemicals & chemical, petroleum & coal products	5.91	4.93	5.14	3.06	3.51
Non-metallic mineral products	2.91	3.20	2.80	1.97	2.13
Basic metals	2.58	3.42	1.66	2.05	2.24
Metal products	3.27	2.85	3.96	1.68	1.64
Other manufacturing	2.78	3.14	2.47		1.92
All manufacturing	3.47	3.62	3.13	2.06	2.00
Mean deviation	.67	.80	.86	.45	.55

Sources:
U.N. Department of Economic and Social Affairs, *Patterns of Industrial Growth, 1938-1958*, New York, 1960, Part II, Statistics and Explanatory Notes for Individual Countries, pp. 153-421.

113

tries, according to the U.N.'s standard industrial classification, for different countries for two or three years covering roughly a time interval from 1938 to 1954. These countries are grouped into four classes according to their degree of industrialization, as measured by value added per head of population[8] during 1953 in manufacturing, stated in current U.S. dollars. We may take either different classes of countries in the same year or an individual country in different years to represent the paths of industrialization in order to detect some general patterns of relative movements of value added per unit of wages and salaries in different industries.

Unfortunately, from this table we can find no evident pattern of industrial differentials in the value added per unit of wages and salaries. Nor can we find any general rule about the relative movements of those ratios over time. We are unable, therefore, to reach any conclusion about the possible biases in employing the wage-bill weights as an approximation to value-added weights.

We know, in theory, that those commodities whose ratios V/r are relatively small would be overweighted and those whose ratios are relatively large would be underweighted if wage-bill weights are used in constructing output indexes. But the industrial differentials of those ratios vary from country to country. The information furnished in Table A-1 does not verify even the general conviction that goods of light industries have smaller value added per unit of wages and salaries than goods of heavy industries. It is very clear in this table that this ratio is much larger in the food, beverages and tobacco industry and the paper and paper products industry than in most of the heavy industries for almost all countries in all years. The explanation of this observation may be either that these two industries are actually capital-intensive rather than labor-intensive, or, more probably, that although they are labor-intensive, wage rates are very low because little skill is required in production in these two industries.

No less obscure are the patterns of relative movements of those ratios over time, or among various classes of countries. Countries in Class I (except Norway), which are countries of highest degree of industrialization so far as manufacturing is concerned, have smaller dispersions of value added per unit of wages and salaries among various manufacturing industries than the countries in the other three classes (except Argentina). However, no striking difference can be found in the dispersions of these ratios in the countries in Classes II, III and IV. The ranges of the

114

highest and the lowest mean deviations in various classes are as follows:

Class I	.23–.40	(Norway: .55–.85)
Class II	.42–.83	(Argentina: .14–.50)
Class III	.42–.74	
Class IV	.45–.86	

This seems to indicate that only in a highly industrialized country does value added per unit of wages and salaries in various industries tend to be equalized.

Looking at the history of development for individual countries in the period studied, the degree of dispersion of the ratios among industries of the following countries has clearly declined, as shown by the decline in the mean deviation:

Australia and the United States in Class I
Union of South Africa in Class II
Japan and Venezuela in Class III

The degree of dispersion has clearly risen in the following countries:

Denmark in Class I
Brazil and India in Class IV

The United Kingdom has had a constant mean deviation for the two years examined. The rest of the countries (5 out of 14 countries studied) have shown fluctuating degrees of dispersion in the development of the economy.

As to the magnitude of value added per unit of wages and salaries for the manufacturing sector as a whole, countries in both Class I and Class II are similar. In these two classes the magnitudes of value added per unit of wages and salaries for the whole manufacturing sector are relatively low and less fluctuating. But they are larger and fluctuate over a wider range for countries in Class III and Class IV. The ranges of the lowest and highest ratio for all manufacturing industry in the four classes are shown as follows:

Class I	1.66–2.36
Class II	1.65–2.74
Class III	2.18–3.39
Class IV	2.00–3.62

The direction of the movement of value added per unit of wages and salaries for the manufacturing sector as a whole is

115

again not the same for all countries studied here. It has clearly declined in:

Denmark, the United Kingdom, and the United States in Class 1
Venezuela in Class III
India in Class IV

It has clearly risen in Argentina (Class II) and Japan (Class III). For the rest of the countries this ratio has fluctuated up and down.

INDUSTRIAL MINISTRIES OF THE CENTRAL GOVERNMENT OF COMMUNIST CHINA

1949	1950	1951	1952	1953	1954
M. of Fuel Industry	Same { B. of Hydro-Electric Engineering, B. of Electricity, B. of Petroleum, B. of Coal Mines }	Same	M. of Fuel Industry	{ B. of Electricity, B. of Coal Mines, B. of Petroleum } Same	Same
M. of Heavy Industry	Same { B. of Steel and Iron Industry, B. of Machinery Industry, B. of Nonferrous Metal Industry, B. of Chemical Industry, B. of Ship-building Industry }	Same	M. of Heavy Industry	{ Anshan Steel and Iron Works, B. of Steel Industry, B. of Nonferrous Metal Industry, B. of Chemical Industry, B. of Building Materials Industry } Same	Same
M. of Textile Industry	Same	Same	First M. of Machinery Industry Second M. of Machinery Industry M. of Textile Industry	Same Same Same	Same Same Same
M. of Light Industry	M. of Light Industry { D. of Paper Industry, D. of Food Industry, D. of Light Industry }	Same	M. of Light Industry	Same	Same
M. of Food Industry				M. of Local Industry	

117

1955	1956	1957	1958	1959	1960
M. of Electric Industry	M. of Electric Industry	Same	M. of Water Conservancy and Electricity	Same	Same
M. of Coal Industry	M. of Coal Industry	Same	Same	Same	Same
M. of Petroleum Industry	M. of Petroleum Industry	Same	Same	Same	Same
	M. of Metallurgy Industry	Same	Same	Same	Same
	M. of Chemical Industry	Same	Same	Same	Same
M. of Heavy Industry	M. of Building Material Industry	Same			
First M. of Machinery Industry	First M. of Machinery Industry	Same	First M. of Machinery Industry	First M. of Machinery Industry	Same
				M. of Agricultural Machine Industry	Same
Second M. of Machinery Industry	Second M. of Machinery Industry	Same	Second M. of Machinery Industry	Second M. of Machinery Industry	Same
Third M. of Machinery Industry		Third M. of Machinery Industry			Third M. of Machinery Industry

APPENDIX B (*continued*)

1955	1956	1957	1958	1959	1960
M. of Textile Industry	M. of Electric Machinery Industry				
M. of Light Industry	M. of Textile Industry	Same	Same	Same	Same
M. of Local Industry	M. of Light Industry	Same	Same	Same	Same
	M. of Food Industry	Same			
	M. of Forest Industry	Same			
	M. of Aquatic Products	Same	Same	Same	Same

Sources:

(1) *People's Handbook, 1950*, Ta Kung Pao, 1950, Shanghai, p. C-1.
(2) *People's Handbook, 1951*, Ta Kung Pao, 1951, Shanghai, Vol. 1, p. D-2.
(3) Chou Fang, *State Organizations of Our Country*, China's Youth Publishing Co., 1955, Peking, pp. 19 and 74.
(4) Hsiang Li, *Governmental Organization of Communist China*, Union Press, 1954, Hong Kong.
(5) *People's Handbook, 1955*, Ta Kung Pao, 1955, Shanghai, pp. 117, 216, and 275.
(6) *People's Handbook, 1956*, Ta Kung Pao, 1956, Tientsin, pp. 241 and 249.
(7) *People's Handbook, 1957*, Ta Kung Pao, 1957, Peking, pp. 310 and 321.
(8) *JMJP*, Feb. 12, 1958.
(9) *TKP*, Feb. 12, 1958.
(10) *JMJP*, Aug. 28, 1959.
(11) *JMJP*, Sept. 14, 1959.

Notes:

M = Ministry (Pu)
B = Bureau (Chu)
D = Department (Chu)

119

Statistical Data

TABLE C-1

PHYSICAL OUTPUT OF INDUSTRIAL COMMODITIES OF COMMUNIST CHINA

Code Number	Commodity	Unit	1949	1950	1951	1952	1953	1954
1.1	Electric Power	Ml.KWH	4310	4550	5750	7260	9200	11000
2.1	Coal	Th.T	32430	42920	53090	66490	69680	83660
2.1.1	Coal Produced in F	Th.T	30984	41010	50720	63528	66572	79505
2.1.2	Coal Produced by H	Th.T	1446	1910	2370	2962	3108	4155
3.1	Crude Petroleum	Th.T	121	200	305	436	622	789
3.1.1	Natural Petroleum	Th.T				195		
3.1.2	Synthetic Petroleum	Th.T				240		
3.2	Gasoline	Th.T						
3.3	Kerosene	Th.T						
3.4	Diesel Oil	Th.T						
4.1	Steel Ingots	Th.T	158	606	896	1349	1774	2225
4.1.1	Steel Ingots Produced by F	Th.T	158	606	896	1349	1774	2225
4.1.2	Steel Ingots Produced by H	Th.T	0	0	0	0	0	0
4.2	Rolled Steel	Th.T	141	464	808	1312	1754	1965
4.3	Pig Iron	Th.T	252	978	1448	1929	2234	3114
4.3.1	Pig Iron Produced in F	Th.T	246	958	1420	1878	2175	3034

Notes:
F = factories.
H = handicrafts.

TABLE C-1 (continued)

Code Number	Commodity	Unit	1949	1950	1951	1952	1953	1954
4.3.2	Pig Iron Produced by H.	Th.T	6	20	28	50	59	79
4.4	Iron Ore	Th.T	589	2350	2703	4287	5821	7229
4.5	Manganese	Th.T	0.7	88	112	191	195	172
4.6	Coke	Th.T			1946	2860	3604	4541
4.6.1	Metallurgical Coke	Th.T		1200	1540	2000	2548	3056
4.6.2	Other Coke	Th.T			406	860	1056	1485
5.1	Aluminum	Th.T	0	0	0	0		
6.1	Metal Cutting Machines	Unit	1582	3312	5853	13734	20502	15901
		Tons				16298	24039	22762
6.2	Power Machinery	Th.H.P.			26	35	144	172
6.2.1	Internal Combustion Engines	Unit				1528		
		Th.H.P.	10	11		28		
6.2.1.1	Diesel Engines	Th.H.P.				18		
6.2.2	Steam Engines	Th.H.P.				7		
6.3	Steam Turbines	Unit			0	0		
		Th.Kc.				11		
6.4	Water Turbines	Unit				7	17	
		Th.Kc.						
6.5	Electric Motors, A.C.	Th.Kc.				91147		
		Unit	61	199	225	639	918	957
6.6	A.C. Generators	Th.Kc.			697	746		
		Unit	10	23	32	30	59	55
6.7	Power Generating Equipment	Th.Kc.	0	0	0	0	0	0
6.8	Boilers (Capacity)	Unit				1000		
		Tons	209	479	782	1222	2270	2361

TABLE C-1 (continued)

Code Number	Commodity	Unit	1949	1950	1951	1952	1953	1954
6.9	Locomotives	Unit	0	0	0	20	10	52
6.10	R.R. Freight Cars	Unit	3155	696	2882	5792	4500	5445
6.11	Passenger Cars	Unit				6		
6.12	Motor Vehicles (Trucks)	Unit	0	0	0	0	0	0
6.13	Trailers	Unit						
6.14	Tractors (Standard Sets)	Unit	0	0	0	0	0	0
6.15	Combine Harvesters	Unit	0	0	0	0	0	0
6.16	Seeders	Unit						
6.17	Plows (Double-Wheel Double Blade)	Unit				344	4590	12469
6.18	Ball Bearings	Th. Sets	138	414	371	5060	3000	60000
6.19	Transformers	Th.V.A.				1179	2181	3795
		Unit				1167079	1960692	1960692
6.20	Merchant Vessels	1000 dwt.T	0	0	0		35	62
6.21	Pumps	Unit				16185		
6.22	Spindles	Th. Sets	0	0	133	383	287	498
6.23	Looms	Unit	0	0	4217	6468	9653	15120
6.24	Paper-Manufacturing Equipment	Th.T						
6.25	Sugar-Manufacturing Equipment	Th.T						
6.26	Metallurgical Equipment	Th.T						
6.27	Bicycles	Th. Units	14	21	44	80	165	298
6.28	Adding Machines	Unit				25	263	1500
6.29	Typewriters	Unit				1556		

TABLE C-1 (*continued*)

Code Number	Commodity	Unit	1949	1950	1951	1952	1953	1954
6.30	Sewing Machines	Th. Sets				84	257	316
6.31	Radios					17071		
6.32	Clocks	Th. Sets				152	306	578
7.1	Ammonium Sulphate	Th.T	27	70	129	181	226	298
7.2	Ammonium Nitrate	Th.T			5	7	23	27
7.3	Phosphorous Fertilizer	Th.T					0	1
7.4	Sulphuric Acid	Th.T	40	49	149	190	260	344
7.5	Soda Ash	Th.T	88	160	185	192	223	309
7.6	Caustic Soda	Th.T	15	23	48	79	88	115
7.7	Sulphur Black	Th.T				16		
7.8	Tires	Th.	26	66	227	417	488	701
7.9	Penicillin	Kg.	0	0	0	46	593	2189
7.10	Insecticide (666 crude powder)	Ton				600		
7.11	Phenol welding powder	Ton						
7.12	Hydrochloric Acid	Th.T						
7.13	Antibiotics	Ton	0	0	0	0		
8.1	Cement	Th.T	660	1410	2490	2860	3880	4600
8.2	Glass Plate	Th.m²	10800	15600	18068	21320	24305	31353
8.3	Asbestos	Ton	119			238		
8.4	Bricks	Bl.						
8.5	Tiles	Ml.						
9.1	Timber	Th.m³	5670	6640	7640	11200	17530	22210
10.1	Cotton Yarn	Th. Bales	1800	2410	2680	3620	4100	4600
10.2	Cotton Cloth	Ml.M	2152	2793	3345	4158	5002	5541

TABLE C-1 (*continued*)

Code Number	Commodity	Unit	1949	1950	1951	1952	1953	1954
10.2.1	Cotton Cloth Produced in F.	Ml.M	1890	2520	3060	3830	4690	5230
10.2.2	Cotton Cloth Produced by H.	Ml.M	262	273	285	329	317	311
10.2.3	Colored and Printed Cloth	Ml.M				1924	2743	3134
10.2.3.1	Print Cloth Produced in F.	Ml.M				1875	2694	3085
10.2.3.2	Print Cloth Produced by H.	Ml.M				49	49	48
10.3	Gunny Sacks	Th. Pieces	9730	15331	39033	67353	59077	59064
10.4	Woolen Fabrics	Th.M	5435	4880	4025	4233	6227	7823
10.5	Woolen Yarn	Ton	1760	1246	801	1980	3718	3273
10.6	Woolen Blankets	Th. Pieces	222	485	1083	717	393	712
10.7	Domesticated Silk	Ton	479	2002	2932	3548	4319	4607
10.8	Tassah Silk	Ton	61	241	444	504	707	546
10.9	Silk Fabrics	Ml.M	50	51	63	65	74	78
10.10	Cotton Undervests	Th. Dozens				2875		
10.11	Socks	Th. Dozens				29930		
10.12	Coats & Pants	Th. Dozens				800		
10.13	Cotton Underwear	Th. Dozens				1898		
10.14	Towels	Th. Dozens				18640		
10.15	Ramie cloth	Ml.M	10.9					
11.1	Paper	Th.T	228	380	492	539	667	842
11.1.1	Machine-made Paper	Th.T	108	141	241	372	427	518
11.1.1.1	Newsprint	Th.T	15	29	53	61	88	85
11.1.1.2	Cigarette Paper	Tons				5028	6338	10487
11.1.1.3	Cardboard	Th.T				17	26	85

TABLE C-1 (*continued*)

Code Number	Commodity	Unit	1949	1950	1951	1952	1953	1954
11.1.2	Paper Produced by H.	Th.T	120	239	251	232	240	324
12.1	Sugar	Th.T	199	242	300	451	638	693
12.1.1	Machine-made Sugar	Th.T	101	122	153	249	298	347
12.1.2	Sugar Produced by H.	Th.T	98	120	147	202	340	346
12.2	Salt	Th.T	2985	2464	4346	4945	3569	4886
12.3	Cigarettes	Th. Crates	1600	1848	2002	2650	3552	3728
12.4	Edible Vegetable Oil	Th.T	444	607	731	983	1009	1066
12.5	Flour	Th.T	1279	1219	1886	2990	3390	3724
12.6	Alcoholic Beverage	Th.T	15			682		
12.7	Alcohol	Th.T				21		
12.8	Beer	Ton				624		
12.9	Dairy Products	Ton				463		
12.9.1	Powdered Milk	Ton						
12.9.2	Condensed Milk	Ton						
12.9.3	Butter	Ton						
12.9.4	Cream Candies	Ton						
12.9.5	Cheese	Ton						
12.10	Milk Substitutes	Ton				426		
12.11	Canned Food	Th.T				14.4		
12.12	Soap	Th.T				117		
13.1	Rubber Footwear	Th. Pairs	28900	45670	65060	61690	76360	85840
13.2	Matches	Th. Baskets	6748	5871	7220	9110	8017	10342
13.3	Light Leather	Th.m²				198716		
13.4	Heavy Leather	Ton				5328		
13.5	Chinaware & Crockery	Th. Pieces				16238	26403	996850
13.6	Enamel Cups	Th.				8241	12230	33981
13.7	Enamel Wash Basins	Th.						18944

TABLE C-1 (*continued*)

Code Number	Commodity	Unit	1949	1950	1951	1952	1953	1954
13.8	Pencils	Th.				148262	198226	230339
13.9	Fountain Pens	Th.				39498	70701	40370
13.10	Thermos Bottles	Th.				5536	12007	14841
13.11	Violins	Unit				5778		
13.12	Accordians	Unit				734		
13.13	Organs	Sets				4781		
14.1	Aquatic Products	Th.T	448	912	1332	1666	1900	2293

Code Number	Commodity	Unit	1955	1956	1957	1958	1959
1.1	Electric Power	Ml.KWH	12280	16590	19340	27530	41500
2.1	Coal	Th.T	98300	110360	130000	270000	347800
2.1.1	Coal Produced in F.	Th.T	93606	105922	123230		
2.1.2	Coal Produced by H.	Th.T	4694	4438	6770		
3.1	Crude Petroleum	Th.T	966	1163	1458	2264	3688
3.1.1	Natural Petroleum	Th.T		589	850	1472	
3.1.2	Synthetic Petroleum	Th.T		574	608	792	
3.2	Gasoline	Th.T		417			
3.3	Kerosene	Th.T		193			
3.4	Diesel Oil	Th.T		323			
4.1	Steel Ingots	Th.T	2853	4465	5350	11080	
4.1.1	Steel Ingots Produced in F.	Th.T	2853	4465	5350	8000	13350
4.1.2	Steel Ingots Produced by H.	Th.T	0	0	0	3080	

TABLE C-1 (continued)

Code Number	Commodity	Unit	1955	1956	1957	1958	1959
4.2	Rolled Steel	Th.T	2505	3921	4478	7208	
4.3	Pig Iron	Th.T	3872	4826	5936	13690	
4.3.1	Pig Iron Produced in F.	Th.T	3794	4777	5887	9530	20522
4.3.2	Pig Iron Produced by H.	Th.T	78	49	49	4160	
4.4	Iron Ore	Th.T	9597	15484	15000		
4.5	Manganese	Th.T	277	524			
4.6	Coke	Th.T	3658	5570	8000	23000	
4.6.1	Metallurgical Coke	Th.T		4243	5040		
4.6.2	Other Coke	Th.T		1327	2960		
5.1	Aluminum	Th.T			29.8	49.8	70.4
6.1	Metal Cutting Machines	Unit	13708	25928	28000	50000	70000
6.2	Power Machinery	Tons	247	657	690	2000	
6.2.1	Internal Combustion Engines	Th.H.P.	21496	29234	609		
		Unit		541			
6.2.1.1	Diesel Engines	Th.H.P.		23			
6.2.2	Steam Engines	Th.H.P.		121			
6.3	Steam Turbines	Unit		57			
		Th.Kc.		103			
6.4	Water Turbines	Unit					
6.5	Electric Motors, A.C.	Th.Kc.	607	1069	1455	6052	
		Unit	107387	184571			
6.6	A.C. Generators	Th.Kc.	108	288		1380	
		Unit	2517	6883			

127

TABLE C-1 (continued)

Code Number	Commodity	Unit	1955	1956	1957	1958	1959
6.7	Power Generating Equipment	Th.Kc.	0	0	198	800	2150
6.8	Boilers	Unit	1274	1035			
	(Capacity)	Tons	2059	3022			
6.9	Locomotives	Unit	98	184	167	350	650
6.10	R.R. Freight Cars	Unit	9258	7122	7300	11000	30000
6.11	Passenger Cars	Unit		311			
6.12	Motor Vehicles (Trucks)	Unit					
6.13	Trailers	Unit	0	1654	7500	16000	15500
6.14	Tractors (Standard Sets)	Unit				30000	
6.15	Combine Harvesters	Unit	0	0	0	957	5598
6.16	Seeders	Unit	3	22	124	545	1250
6.17	Plows (Double-Wheel Double Blade)	Unit	24533	74299			
6.18	Ball Bearings	Th. Sets	524000	1793186			
6.19	Transformers	Th.V.A.	1925989	2891070			
		Unit	55660	110514			
6.20	Merchant Vessels	1000 dwt.T	120	104	54	90	122
6.21	Pumps	Unit	37397	784	484	1000	1400
6.22	Spindles	Th. Sets	304		10420	13680	21900
6.23	Looms	Unit	9291	19251			
6.24	Paper-Manufacturing Equipment	Th.T			7	15	
6.25	Sugar-Manufacturing Equipment	Th.T			9	15	

TABLE C-1 (*continued*)

Code Number	Commodity	Unit	1955	1956	1957	1958	1959
6.26	Metallurgical Equipment	Th.T			16	110	205
6.27	Bicycles	Th. Units	335	640	806	1174	1498
6.28	Adding Machines	Unit	2424	5060	6950		
6.29	Typewriters	Unit			8560		
6.30	Sewing Machines	Th. Sets	174	206	267	637	563
6.31	Radios	Unit	70000	125300	295300		
6.32	Clocks	Th.	812	1699	2033	3068	5700
7.1	Ammonium Sulphate	Th.T	332	523	631	811	1333
7.2	Ammonium Nitrate	Th.T			120	307	
7.3	Phosphorous Fertilizer	Th.T	21	78	120	344	1056
7.4	Sulphuric Acid	Th.T	375	517	632	740	851
7.5	Soda Ash	Th.T	405	476	506	640	360
7.6	Caustic Soda	Th.T	137	156	198	270	
7.7	Sulfur Black	Th.T					
7.8	Tires	Th.	593	783	873	1747	
7.9	Penicillin	Kg.	7829	14037	18266	72607	
7.10	Insecticide (666 crude powder)	Ton		50000		65000	133000
7.11	Phenol welding powder	Ton		7800			
7.12	Hydrochloric Acid	Th.T				113	
7.13	Antibiotics	Ton			34.6	145	198
8.1	Cement	Th.T	4500	6390	6860	9300	12270
8.2	Glass Plate	Th.m^2	27716	30750	51776	52670	
8.3	Asbestos	Ton			1473	3035	
8.4	Bricks	Bl.			21	40	

TABLE C-1 (*continued*)

Code Number	Commodity	Unit	1955	1956	1957	1958	1959
8.5	Tiles	Ml.			3300	5000	
9.1	Timber	Th.m³	20930	20840	27870	35000	41200
10.1	Cotton Yarn	Th. Bales	3970	5250	4650	6100	8250
10.2	Cotton Cloth	Ml.M	4510	5844			
10.2.1	Cotton Cloth Produced in F.	Ml.M	4360	5770	5050	5700	7500
10.2.2	Cotton Cloth Produced by H.	Ml.M	149	74			
10.2.3	Colored and Printed Cloth	Ml.M	2753	3273	2768	3460	
10.2.3.1	Print Cloth Produced in F.	Ml.M	2709	3188			
10.2.3.2	Print Cloth Produced by H.	Ml.M	44	85			
10.3	Gunny Sacks	Th. Pieces	52605	78683	84560	115000	
10.4	Woolen Fabrics	Th.M	10271	14267	16190	26400	31100
10.5	Woolen Yarn	Ton	3743	5658	5200	9540	
10.6	Woolen Blankets	Th. Pieces	784	920	5847	7250	
10.7	Domesticated Silk	Ton	5377	6191	3636	3750	
10.8	Tassah Silk	Ton	587	1337	145	200	
10.9	Silk Fabrics	Ml.M	94	119			264
10.10	Cotton Undervests	Th. Dozens			9566		
10.11	Socks	Th. Dozens			36463		
10.12	Coats & Pants	Th. Dozens			1926		
10.13	Cotton Underwear	Th. Dozens			4091		
10.14	Towels	Th. Dozens			23375		
10.15	Ramie Cloth	Ml.M		23	35		

TABLE C-1 (continued)

Code Number	Commodity	Unit	1955	1956	1957	1958	1959
11.1	Paper	Th.T	839	998	1221	1630	2137
11.1.1	Machine-made Paper	Th.T	575	729	913	1220	1700
11.1.1.1	Newsprint	Th.T	89	103	122		
11.1.1.2	Cigarette Paper	Tons	6973	9574	8803		
11.1.1.3	Cardboard	Th.T	137	158	195		
11.1.2	Paper Produced by H.	Th.T	264	269	308	348	
12.1	Sugar	Th.T	717	807	864	900	1130
12.1.1	Machine-made Sugar	Th.T	410	518	558		
12.1.2	Sugar Produced by H.	Th.T	307	289	306		
12.2	Salt	Th.T	7535	4940	8277	10400	11040
12.3	Cigarettes	Th. Crates	3567	3907	4456	4750	5505
12.4	Edible Vegetable Oil	Th.T	1165	1076	1100	1250	1466
12.5	Flour	Th.T	4530	4519	5030		
12.6	Alcoholic Beverage	Th.T	852	1098	749	1091	
12.7	Alcohol	Th.T		58	61	120	
12.8	Beer	Ton			53		
12.9	Dairy Products	Ton		6437	10863		
12.9.1	Powdered Milk	Ton			4520		
12.9.2	Condensed Milk	Ton			4769		
12.9.3	Butter	Ton			836		
12.9.4	Cream Candies	Ton			336		
12.9.5	Cheese	Ton			402		
12.10	Milk Substitutes	Ton			7616		
12.11	Canned Food	Th.T		28.8	50.8		
12.12	Soap	Th.T		260	242	272	

TABLE C-1 (*continued*)

Code Number	Commodity	Unit	1955	1956	1957	1958	1959
13.1	Rubber Footwear	Th. Pairs	97450	103480	128850	182360	
13.2	Matches	Th. Baskets	11904	11597	10350	11070	
13.3	Light Leather	Th.m²			977260		
13.4	Heavy Leather	Ton			15204		
13.5	Chinaware & Crockery	Th. Pieces			1621560		
13.6	Enamel Cups	Th.	20660	25123	26237		
13.7	Enamel Wash Basins	Th.	25479	20816	19706		
13.8	Pencils	Th.	179894	309598	484760		
13.9	Fountain Pens	Th.	34678	47058	52000	80670	130000
13.10	Thermos Bottles	Th.	17958	16310	20870	27611	37000
13.11	Violins	Unit			70025		
13.12	Accordians	Unit			22679		
13.13	Organs	Sets			21365		
14.1	Aquatic Products	Th.T	2518	2648	3120	4060	5020

Notes:
 F = factories.
 H = handicrafts.

132

Statistical Data

Sources of Output Data in Table C-1

(1) Output figures of the following items for 1949-1958 are taken from
TGY, pp. 95-100:

1.1	2.1	3.1	4.1	4.1.2	4.3	6.1
6.2	6.5	6.7	6.9	6.12	6.14	6.15
6.20	6.27	7.1	7.4	7.5	7.9	8.1
9.1	10.1	10.2.1	11.1	12.1	12.2	12.3
12.4	13.1	14.1				

(2) 1959 output figures of the following items are from Li Fuchun, "Report
on the Draft of National Economic Plan for 1960," *JMJP*, March 21, 1960.

1.1	2.1	3.1	4.1.1	4.3.1	6.1	6.7
6.26	7.4	8.1	9.1	10.1	10.2.1	11.1
11.1.1	12.2	12.3	12.4	14.1		

(3) Output figures of the following items in the indicated years are taken from
CH. The specific page numbers are attached, respectively, to the referred
items.

    4.2   : 1949 to 1956—pp. 11 and 19
    4.3.1 : 1952 to 1956—p. 30
    4.3.2 : 1952 to 1956—p. 30
    4.4   : 1949 to 1956—pp. 11 and 19
    4.5   : 1949 to 1956—pp. 11 and 19

    6.2.1   : 1952 to 1956—p. 123
    6.2.1.1 : 1952—p. 114
    6.2.2   : 1952—p. 142
    6.3   : 1956—p. 122
    6.4   : 1952, 1953 and 1956—p. 122
    6.5   : 1952, 1955 and 1956—pp. 123 and 139
    6.6   : 1949 to 1952—p. 113
    6.6   : 1956—p. 123
    6.6   : 1955—p. 139
    6.8   : 1949 to 1952, and 1956—pp. 113, 123 and 139
    6.10   : 1949 to 1952, and 1956—pp. 113 and 123
    6.11   : 1952 and 1956—p. 123
    6.16   : 1952 and 1956—p. 123
    6.17   : 1952 to 1956—p. 123
    6.18   : 1949 to 1952—p. 113
    6.19   : 1952, and 1954 to 1956—pp. 123 and 139
    6.21   : 1955—p. 129
    6.22   : 1952 to 1956—p. 161
    6.23   : 1949 to 1956—p. 161

    10.2.3   : 1952 to 1956—p. 166
    10.2.2   : 1949 to 1956—pp. 155 & 166
    10.2.3.1 : 1952 to 1956—p. 177
    10.3   : 1949 to 1956—pp. 155 & 166
    10.4   : 1949 to 1956—pp. 155 & 166
    10.5   : 1949 to 1956—pp. 155 & 166
    10.6   : 1949 to 1956—pp. 155 & 166
    10.7   : 1949 to 1956—pp. 155 & 166
    10.8   : 1949 to 1956—pp. 155 & 166
    10.9   : 1950 to 1956—pp. 155 & 166

Sources of Output Data in Table C-1 (*continued*)

11.1.1   : 1949 to 1956—pp. 204 & 206
11.1.1.1 : 1949 to 1957—pp. 204 & 209
11.1.1.2 : 1952 to 1957—p. 209
11.1.1.3 : 1952 to 1957—p. 209

(4) The remaining output data are from scattered sources:

2.1.1   for 1949: *SSB 1954's Communique*
for 1952 to 1955: *TCKTTH* No. 22, 1956
for 1956: *SSB 1956's Communique*
for 1950, 1951 and 1957: *JPRS* 3787, Aug. 31, 1960, p. 10

2.1.2   for all years: by subtracting 2.1.1 from 2.1

3.1.1   for 1956 and 1958: *HCKTKY*, p. 50, and *China News Service*, Sept. 12, 1959
for 1957: *JPRS* 818-D, April 4, 1958, p. 44

3.1.2   for all years: *HCKTKY*, p. 50, and *China News Service*, Sept. 12, 1959

3.2   for all years: *HCKTKY*, p. 50

3.3   for all years: *HCKTKY*, p. 50

3.4   for all years: *HCKTKY*, p. 50

4.1.1   for 1949 to 1957, figures are taken from 4.1 because there were no steel ingots produced by handicrafts prior to 1958. See *CH*, p. 31.
for 1958: *TGY*, p. 95

4.2   for 1957: *TKP*, March 2, 1958
for 1958: I. G. Bukhvostov & Huang Ssu-tsang, "The Development of Rolled Metal Production in the People's Republic of China," *Metallurg*, No. 2, Feb. 1960, Moscow, pp. 37-40.

4.3.1   for 1950 and 1951: the differences between 4.3 and 4.3.2
for 1949: *SSB 1954 Communique*
for 1958: *TGY*, p. 95

4.3.2   for 1949: the difference between 4.3 and 4.3.1
for 1950 and 1951: calculated from the indexes given in *CH*, p. 11
for 1958: *TGY*, p. 95

4.4   for 1957: *TKP*, March 2, 1958

4.6   for all years: calculated from the information given in *SSB 1953 Communique*, *SSB 1952 Communique* (*Revised*), *FFYP*, p. 36, *SSB 1954 Communique*, *People's Handbook*, 1957, p. 442, and *China News Analysis*, June 2, 1961, No. 374, p. 6.

4.6.1   for all years: A. N. Gorodilov, "The Coke-Chemical Industry of the People's Republic of China," *Koks i Khimiya*, No. 10, 1958, Moscow.

4.6.2   for all years: differences between 4.6 and 4.6.1

5.1   for all years: calculated from the information given in *JPRS* 3605 (26 July 1960) p. 48, and *JPRS* 7051 (15 Nov. 1960), p. 16, and *JPRS* 11757 (Jan. 2, 1962), p. 32.

6.1   for 1952 to 1955, stated in units of tonnage: *FFYP*, p. 37; *TCKTTH*, No. 22, 1956; *CC*, pp. 70; and *SSB 1956 Communique*.

Sources of Output Data in Table C-1 (*continued*)

6.2.1	for 1955: in numbers: *HHPYK*, No. 14, 1956, p. 2
	for 1957: in units of H.P.: *SSB 1953-57 Communique*
6.6	for 1953: *SSB 1953 Communique*
	for 1954 and 1955: *SSB 1955 Communique*
	for 1951: in numbers: *SSB 1952 Communique* (*Revised*)
	for 1958: *China News Service*, Sept. 5, 1959
6.8	for 1953 and 1954: *SSB 1953 Communique* and *SSB 1954 Communique*
6.9	for 1959: *JPRS* 13052, March 12, 1962, pp. 8 and 9
6.10	for 1953: *SSB 1954 Communique*
	for 1954 and 1955: *SSB 1955 Communique*
	for 1957: *HHPYK*, No. 7, 1959, p. 58
	for 1959: *JPRS* 13052, March 12, 1962, pp. 8-9
	for 1958: *HHPYK*, No. 9, 1959, p. 16
6.12	for 1959: *JPRS* 13052, March 12, 1962, pp. 8-9.
6.13	for 1958: *Chi-Che* (Motorcars), No. 9, 1959, p. 2
6.14	for 1959: *JMJP*, April 11, 1960
6.15	for 1959: *JMJP*, April 11, 1960
6.16	for 1953 to 1955: *CKKJ*, No. 5, 1958, p. 18
6.17	for 1953 to 1955: *CC*, p. 70
6.18	for 1953: *SSB 1953 Communique*
	for 1954: *SSB 1953 Communique* and *SSB 1954 Communique*
6.19	for 1953 and 1954, in units of V.A.: *SSB 1953 Communique* and *SSB 1954 Communique*
6.20	for 1959: *JPRS* 8116, April 18, 1961, p. 40
6.22	for 1949 to 1951: calculated on the basis of the following information:
	a) Communist China began producing spindles in 1951. See *CH*, p. 161
	b) The total production of spindles during the period from 1951 to 1956 was 2,380,000 units. See *CH*, p. 161
	c) The actual output figures for the years from 1952 to 1956 are given in *CH*, p. 161
	for 1957: *SSB 1953-57 Communique*
	for 1958: *SSB 1958 Communique*
	for 1959: *JMJP*, April 5, 1960
6.23	for 1958 and 1959: *JMJP*, April 5, 1960
6.24	for 1957: *SSB 1953-57 Communique*
	for 1958: *SSB 1958 Communique*
6.25	for 1957: *SSB 1953-57 Communique*
	for 1958: *SSB 1958 Communique*
6.26	for 1957: *JMJP*, Sept. 24, 1959
	for 1958: *China News Service*, Sept. 5, 1959
6.27	for 1959: *JMJP*, Sept. 18, 1959
6.28	for 1952 and 1957: *CKCKY*, No. 20, 1957, p. 2
	for 1953 to 1956: *CKCKY*, No. 16, 1957, pp. 10-13
6.29	for 1952 and 1957: *CKCKY*, No. 20, 1957, p. 2
6.30	for 1952: *CKCKY*, No. 2, 1958, pp. 2-5
	for 1953 to 1956: *CKCKY*, No. 16, 1957, pp. 10-13
	for 1957 & 1958: *CKCKY*, No. 18, 1959, pp. 3-4
	for 1959: *JMJP*, April 7, 1960

Sources of Output Data in Table C-1 (*continued*)

6.31	for 1952 & 1957: *SCYHF*, pp. 56-57
	for 1955 & 1956: *People's Handbook 1958*, p. 460
6.32	for 1952 & 1957: *CKCKY*, No. 2, 1958, pp. 205
	for 1953 to 1956: *CKCKY*, No. 16, 1957, pp. 10-13
	for 1958: *CKCKY*, No. 18, 1959, pp. 3-4
	for 1959: *JMJP*, April 7, 1960
7.1	for 1959: *SSB 1959 Communique*
7.2	for 1951 to 1953: *SSB 1952 Communique* (*Revised*); *SSB 1953 Communique*; and *FFYP*, p. 36
	for 1954: Chang Chen, *The Chemical Industry in the First Five Year Plan*, Chung Hua Chuan Kuo Ko Hsueh Chi Shuo Pu Chi Hsieh Hui, 1956, Peking, p. 25
	for 1957 and 1958: *HHPYK*, No. 5, 1959, p. 104, and *CB*, No. 494, 1958, p. 15
7.3	for 1953 to 1955: *SLFT*, No. 5, 1958, p. 8
	for 1957 and 1958: *Chung Kuo Hsin Wen* (*China News*), No. 1787, Jan. 30, 1959, p. 11
	for 1956: *HHKY*, No. 5, 1957, p. 16
7.5	for 1959: *HHKY*, No. 1, Jan. 1960, pp. 1-2
7.6	for 1959: *JMJP*, April 16, 1960
7.7	for 1952: *FFYP*, p. 36
7.8	for 1949 and 1952 to 1956: *SSB 1955 Communique*; *SSB 1956 Communique* and *SSB 1953-1957 Communique*
	for 1950: Tientsin, *TKP*, Sept. 20, 1954
	for 1951: calculated from the index given in *SSB 1952 Communique* (*Revised*)
	for 1957: *HHKY*, No. 12, 1957, pp. 1-2
	for 1958: *HHKY*, No. 3, 1959, pp. 1-4
7.10	for 1952 and 1956: Chang Chen, *The Chemical Industry in the First Five Year Plan*, p. 29
	for 1958: *HHKY*, No. 18, 1959, pp. 19-21
	for 1959: *NCNA*, Sept. 29, 1960
7.11	for 1956: *Ko Hsueh Hua Pao* (Science Pictorial), No. 3, 1958, pp. 81-83
7.12	for 1958: *KJJP*, Oct. 2, 1959
7.13	for 1957-1959: *JPRS* 11757, Jan. 2, 1962, p. 32
8.2	for 1949 and 1956: *HCKTKY*, p. 52
	for 1950 to 1954: *FFYP*, pp. 36-37; *SSB 1952 Communique* (*Revised*); *SSB 1953 Communique*; *SSB 1954 Communique*; and Fan Ching Pin, *The Essentials of the Chinese Communist Industrial Economy*, Freedom Press, 1953, Hong Kong, p. 21
	for 1955: *JPRS* 333, 1958
	for 1957: obtained by subtracting the production figures of the rest years from the total production in the period from 1953 to 1957, as given in *CCTLKY*, No. 9, 1959, p. 7
	for 1958: *CCTLKY*, No. 9, 1959, pp. 3 and 7
8.3	for 1949, 1952, 1957 and 1958: *CCTLKY*, No. 18, 1959, pp. 18-19
8.4	for 1957 and 1958: *CCTLKY*, No. 1, 1959, p. 10

Statistical Data

Sources of Output Data in Table C-1 (*continued*)

8.5	for 1957 and 1958: *CCTLKY*, No. 1, 1959, p. 10
10.2	for 1952 to 1955: *TCKTTH*, No. 22, 1956 for 1949: *SSB 1954 Communique* for 1950, 1951 and 1956: obtained by adding figures of 10.2.1 and 10.2.2 of each year
10.2.3	for 1957 and 1958: *China Weekly*, No. 388, June 13, 1960, Hong Kong, pp. 18-25
10.2.3.2	for 1952 to 1956: differences between 10.2.3 and 10.2.3.1. They can be checked with the rates of increase in the handicraft production of colored and printed cloth as given in *CH*, p. 167
10.3	for 1957 and 1958: *China Weekly*, No. 388, June 14, 1960, pp. 18-25
10.4	for 1957: *SCYHF*, pp. 56-57 for 1958: *CKFC*, No. 28, Oct. 1, 1959, pp. 17-19 for 1958: *CKFC*, No. 3, 1959, pp. 1-2
10.5	for 1957: *SCYHF*, pp. 56-57 for 1958: *CKFC*, No. 28, Oct. 1, 1959, pp. 17-19
10.7	for 1957 and 1958: *China Weekly*, No. 388, June 13, 1960, pp. 18-25
10.8	for 1957: *CKFC*, No. 4, Feb. 1959, pp. 6-7 for 1958: *CKFC*, No. 28, Oct. 1, 1959, pp. 22-25
10.9	for 1949: *CKFC*, No. 4, Feb. 1959, pp. 6-7 for 1957: *SCYHF*, pp. 56-57 for 1958: *CKFC*, No. 28, Oct. 1, 1959, pp. 22-25
10.10	for 1952 and 1956: *SCYHF*, pp. 56-57
10.11	for 1952 and 1956: *SCYHF*, pp. 56-57
10.12	for 1952 and 1956: *SCYHF*, pp. 56-57
10.13	for 1952 and 1956: *SCYHF*, pp. 56-57
10.14	for 1952 and 1956: *SCYHF*, pp. 56-57
10.15	for all years: *CKFC*, No. 1, 1957, p. 4, and No. 28, 1959, pp. 5-10
11.1.1	for 1957 and 1958: *HHPYK*, No. 10, 1959, p. 36
11.1.2	for 1949 to 1958: *Tsao Chih Kung Yeh* (Paper Industry), No. 2, 1959, p. 47
12.1.1	for 1950: the difference between 12.1 and 12.1.2 for 1952 to 1954: *SSB 1954 Communique* for 1955: *SSB 1955 Communique* for 1956: *SSB 1956 Communique* for 1957: *NCNA*, Peking, Dec. 30, 1957 for 1949 and 1951: calculated from the indexes given in *Ching Chi Nien Pao* (Economic Yearbook), 1954, Ching Chi Tao Pao She, Hong Kong, 1955, p. 4
12.1.2	for 1949 to 1957, except 1952: differences between 12.1 and 12.1.1 for 1952: *HCKTKY*, p. 101
12.5	for 1950 to 1952: *FFYP*, pp. 36-37, *SSB 1952 Communique* (*Revised*) for 1953 to 1955: *TCKTTH*, No. 22, 1956 for 1957: *JPRS* 3234, 1960, pp. 75-76 for 1949 and 1956: *HCKTKY*, p. 57

Sources of Output Data in Table C-1 (*continued*)

12.6	for 1952 and 1957: *SCYHF*, pp. 56-57
	for 1956: *HHPYK*, No. 17, 1957, p. 133
	for 1955: *CKCKY*, No. 10, 1956, pp. 5-9
	for 1958: *Shih Pin Kung Yeh* (Food Industry), No. 18, 1959, p. 2
12.6.1	for 1957: *Shih Pin Kung Yeh*, No. 18, 1959, p. 2
12.7	for 1949, 1952 and 1956: *JPRS 598-D*, (1959)
	for 1957: *HHPYK*, No. 7, 1959, p. 51
	for 1958: *HHPYK*, No. 1, 1959, p. 84
12.9	for 1952 and 1957: *HHPYK*, No. 8, 1958, p. 20
	for 1956: *JPRS 3234* (1960), p. 220
12.9.1	for 1952 and 1957: *HHPYK*, No. 8, 1958, p. 20
12.9.2	for 1957: *HHPYK*, No. 8, 1958, p. 20
12.9.3	for 1957: *HHPYK*, No. 8, 1958, p. 20
12.9.4	for 1957: *HHPYK*, No. 8, 1958, p. 20
12.9.5	for 1957: *HHPYK*, No. 8, 1958, p. 20
12.10	for 1952 and 1957: *HHPYK*, No. 8, 1958, p. 20
12.11	for 1952 and 1957: *SCYHF*, pp. 56-57
	for 1956: *JMJP*, Jan. 15, 1957
12.12	for 1952: *HHPYK*, No. 17, 1957, p. 133
	for 1956 to 1958: *CKCKY*, No. 5, 1959, pp. 3-6
13.2	for 1949 to 1953: *FFYP*, pp. 36-37; *SSB 1952 Communique* (*Revised*); and *SSB 1953 Communique*
	for 1954: *SSB 1954 Communique*
	for 1955: *CKCKY*, No. 16, 1957, pp. 10-13
	for 1956: *JPRS 3234* (1960), pp. 75-76
	for 1957 and 1958: *CKCKY*, No. 5, 1959, pp. 3-6
13.3	for 1952 and 1957: *CKCKY*, No. 20, 1957, p. 2
13.4	for 1952 and 1957: *CKCKY*, No. 20, 1957, p. 2
13.5	for 1954 and 1957: *CKCKY*, No. 20, 1957, p. 2
13.6	for 1952: *CKCKY*, No. 20, 1957, p. 2
	for 1953 to 1956: *CKCKY*, No. 16, 1957, p. 13
	for 1957: *SCYHF*, pp. 56-57
13.7	for 1952: *CKCKY*, No. 20, 1957, p. 2
	for 1953 to 1956: *CKCKY*, No. 16, 1957, p. 13
	for 1957: *SCYHF*, pp. 56-57
13.8	for 1952: *CKCKY*, No. 20, 1957, p. 2
	for 1953 to 1956: *CKCKY*, No. 16, 1957, p. 13
	for 1957: *SCYHF*, pp. 56-57
13.9	for 1952: *CKCKY*, No. 20, 1957, p. 2
	for 1953 to 1956: *CKCKY*, No. 16, 1957, p. 13
	for 1957 and 1958: *CKCKY*, No. 18, 1959, pp. 3-4
	for 1959: *JMJP*, April 7, 1960
13.10	for 1952: *CKCKY*, No. 20, 1957, p. 2
	for 1953 to 1956: *CKCKY*, No. 16, 1957, p. 13
	for 1957 and 1958: *CKCKY*, No. 5, 1959, pp. 3-6
	for 1959: *JMJP*, April 7, 1960
13.11	for 1952 and 1957: *CKCKY*, No. 20, 1957, p. 2
13.12	for 1952 and 1957: *CKCKY*, No. 2, 1958, pp. 2-5
13.13	for 1952 and 1957: *CKCKY*, No. 20, 1957, p. 2

Statistical Data

TABLE C-2
INDEXES OF OUTPUT OF NONFERROUS METALS, 1951-1959
(1952 or 1957=100)

	Copper	Lead	Zinc	Tungsten	Tin	Aluminum*
1951	75	70	n.a.	n.a.	n.a.	0
1952	100	100	100	100	100	0
1953	136	176	150	n.a.	109	0
1954	157	316	196	n.a.	n.a.	n.a.
1955	160	290	250	142	n.a.	n.a.
1956	n.a.	n.a.	n.a.	n.a.	n.a.	n.a.
1957	327	450	305	n.a.	n.a.	100
1958	n.a.	n.a.	n.a.	n.a.	n.a.	169
1959	n.a.	n.a.	n.a.	n.a.	n.a.	237

Sources:

For copper and lead in 1951 and all figures in 1953, from *SSB 1952's Communique* (*revised*) and *SSB 1953's Communique*.

For all figures in 1954, from *SSB 1954's Communique*.

For all figures in 1952 and 1955, from Sung Yang-chu, *The Metallurgical Industry in the First Five Year Plan*, Peking, 1955, p. 27.

For all figures except that of aluminum in 1957, from *JPRS* 3234, May 23, 1960, p. 136.

For figures of aluminum, from *Yeh Chin Poo* (Metallurgical Bulletin), No. 44, 1959, pp. 69-71 and No. 46, 1959, pp. 28-31.

* No aluminum was produced in 1952, and 1957 is taken as the comparison base.

TABLE C-3
GROSS OUTPUT VALUE OF THE NONFERROUS METAL INDUSTRY, 1949-1957
(At 1952 Constant Prices)

	Gross Output Value (in million yuan)	Index (1952=100)
1949	107	17.4
1950	n.a.	n.a.
1951	n.a.	n.a.
1952	614	100.0
1953	n.a.	n.a.
1954	n.a.	n.a.
1955	1271	207.1
1956	n.a.	n.a.
1957	2271	370.0

Sources:

For 1949 and 1952, from *CH*, p. 53.
For 1955, from *HHPYK*, 1957, No. 1, p. 68.
For 1957, from *CHCC*, 1958, No. 3, p. 10.

TABLE C-4

Factory Production and Handicraft Production of Selected Commodities, 1949-1957

Commodity		Unit	1949	1950	1951	1952	1953	1954	1955	1956	1957
Coal	(F)	1000 tons	30,984	41,010	50,720	63,528	66,572	79,505	93,606	105,922	123,230
	(H)	1000 tons	1,446	1,910	2,370	2,962	3,108	4,155	4,694	4,438	6,770
Pig iron	(F)	1000 tons	246	958	1,420	1,878	2,175	3,034	3,794	4,777	5,887
	(H)	1000 tons	6	20	28	50	59	79	78	49	49
Timber	(F)	1000 M³	3,750	4,500	5,980	10,020	15,230	17,810	12,500	10,700	20,000
	(H)	1000 M³	1,920	2,140	1,660	1,180	2,300	4,400	8,430	10,140	7,870
Cotton cloth	(F)	million M	1,890	2,520	3,060	3,830	4,690	5,230	4,360	5,770	5,050
	(H)	million M	262	273	285	329	317	311	149	74	67
Print cloth	(F)	million M	926	1,233	1,498	1,875	2,694	3,085	2,709	3,188	2,790
	(H)	million M	24	32	40	49	49	48	44	85	74
Silk fabrics	(F)	million M	30	31	38	39	52	60	80	109	139
	(H)	million M	20	20	25	26	22	18	14	10	6
Paper	(F)	1000 tons	108	141	241	372	427	518	575	729	913
	(H)	1000 tons	102	239	251	167	240	324	264	269	308
Sugar	(F)	1000 tons	101	122	153	249	298	347	410	518	558
	(H)	1000 tons	98	120	147	202	340	346	307	289	306
Salt	(F)	1000 tons	2,089	1,724	3,041	3,460	2,034	3,306	5,900	3,832	6,421
	(H)	1000 tons	896	740	1,305	1,485	1,535	1,580	1,635	1,108	1,856
Edible Vegetable Oil	(F)	1000 tons	278	380	458	724	890	941	1,015	895	883
	(H)	1000 tons	166	227	273	259	119	125	150	181	217

Notes:

F = factory output.

H = handicraft output.

TABLE C-4 (continued)

Sources and estimation procedures:

Coal: Handicraft output and non-handicraft (factory) output are officially given for all years. (See Table C-1).

Pig iron: Handicraft output and factory output are known for 1949 and 1952 to 1956. Figures for handicraft production for 1950 and 1951 are estimated from the index numbers given in *CH*, p. 11. Handicraft output of pig iron rose steadily from 1949 to 1954 but sharply declined in 1956, perhaps due to the strengthened socialization of handicrafts since 1955. With no information available we assume that the handicraft output of pig iron in 1957 remained the same as that in 1956. The differences between total output and handicraft output are taken as factory output for 1950, 1951 and 1957. A few words ought to be said about the 1958 figures. In early 1959 the Communist authorities announced that production of steel ingots in 1958 was 11,080,000 tons and pig iron output was 13,690,000 tons. However, a few months later they revised the figures of steel output and pig iron output in 1958 by claiming that 3,080,000 tons out of the 11,080,000 tons of steel and 4,160,000 tons out of the 13,690,000 tons of pig iron were produced by "indigenous methods" and should be separated from the production figures of ordinary steel and pig iron. Some troubles arose in dealing with this year's figures, as an outcome of the announced revision of production data. First of all, in official statistical practice handicraft production is defined not according to the method of production but according to whether hired workers are employed by the producing units. As we have seen, output of handicraft factories is included in "factory production" rather than "handicraft production," though these factories are using "indigenous methods" in their production. Therefore, the output by "indigenous methods" is not conceptually identical to the output of "handicrafts." Secondly, it is doubtful whether that 3,080,000 tons of steel actually existed. This figure could be completely fictitious for something nonexistent or utterly useless; and to describe it as applicable to indigenous steel instead of making an outright confession—as in the case of grain production in that year—of the exaggeration by individual reporting units could be merely a face-saving device. This possibility is even clearer if one examines the figures for pig iron production in 1958, which were revised in the same manner as those for steel production. The figures for pig iron output for the years from 1949 to 1957 given on p. 95 of *TGY* are the total output figures of both factory production and handicraft production. But in the same table pig iron production in 1958 was separated into "indigenous pig iron" and "regular pig iron." If "indigenous pig iron" in 1958 were the same as that in the previous years, why should it be singled out particularly for 1958? It is also interesting to note that the categories of "indigenous steel" and "indigenous pig iron" entirely disappeared from all official reports of 1959's economic achievements despite the fact that not all the backyard furnaces were converted into modern ones. Based on all these considerations, it is decided that the reported 3,080,000 tons of steel and 4,160,000 tons of pig iron "produced by indigenous methods" in 1958 are to be ignored in our computations.

Timber: The actual factory output and handicraft output are directly given or can be calculated for 1949, 1950, 1952 and 1955 to 1957. (For 1949 and 1950, see *HHYP*, April 1951, p. 1330 and July 1951, p. 659; for 1952, see *FFYP*, p. 37; for 1955 and 1956, see C. M. Li, *Economic Development of Communist China*, p. 44; and for 1957, see *HCKTKY*, p. 52). Figures of handicraft output for 1951, 1953 and 1954 are interpolated.

Sources and estimation procedures (*continued*)

Cotton cloth: All figures are known except 1957's handicraft output. According to one Communist source (*CKFC*, 1957, No. 16, p. 21), with 1952 as 100, the cotton yarn consumptions for handicraft cloth in 1956 and 1957 are 149.73 and 135.16 respectively, indicating a decline of 9% from 1956 to 1957. Output of handicraft cloth for 1957 is estimated by assuming that it also declined by 9% in that year.

Print cloth: Factory output and handicraft output are known for the years from 1952 to 1956. For other years, factory outputs are extrapolated on the basis of rates of increase in factory production of cotton cloth. To estimate handicraft outputs, we have assumed that the proportion of handicraft output to factory output in 1949-51 was the same as in 1952 and the 1956's proportion remained the same in 1957.

Silk fabrics: Handicraft output is known for 1952 and 1957 (*FFYP*, p. 64 and *CKFC*, 1958, No. 2, p. 3). Handicraft outputs for 1953-56 are interpolated while that for 1949-51 are estimated by using the proportion of handicraft output to total silk fabrics in 1952. Factory outputs in various years are the differences between total outputs and estimated handicraft outputs in those years.

Paper: Handicraft output and factory output are known for all years.

Sugar: Handicraft output and factory output are known for all years.

Salt: Handicraft output is known for 1952, 1955 and 1956 (*FFYP*, p. 38 and *JMJP*, Feb. 26, 1957). Interpolation is made to estimate handicraft output for 1953 and 1954. The proportion of handicraft output to total salt production in 1952 is used to estimate handicraft output for 1949-51; and 1956's proportion is used to estimate 1957's handicraft output. The differences between total outputs and estimated handicraft outputs in various years are taken as factory outputs in those years.

Edible vegetable oil: Handicraft output is known for the years 1951-54 and 1957 (*FFYP*, pp. 37-38 and *SPKY*, 1957, No. 10, p. 291). 1955 and 1956's handicraft outputs are estimated by interpolation while that for 1949 and 1950 are estimated by using the proportion of handicraft output to total output in 1951. The differences between total output and handicraft output are taken as factory outputs in those years.

TABLE C-5

PRICE WEIGHTS USED IN COMPUTING THE INDEX OF HANDICRAFT PRODUCTION

Item	Unit	Price (yuan)	Remark and Source
Coal	ton	18.60	Medium price, *TTJP*, Jan. 2, 1952
Pig iron	ton	135.00	Lowest price, 4.3.1 in Table C-9
Timber	m³	116.00	Medium price, *KYCT*, Jan. 1952, p. 42
Cotton cloth	m	0.60	Lowest price, 10.2.1 in Table C-9
Print cloth	m	0.84	Lowest price, *TTJP*, Jan. 2, 1952
Silk fabrics	m	3.20	Lowest price, 10.9.1 in Table C-9
Paper	ton	500.00	Mao-pien paper, *CFJP*, Jan. 4, 1952
Sugar	ton	840.00	Lowest price, 12.1.1 in Table C-9
Salt	ton	183.00	Lowest price, 12.2.1 in Table C-9
Edible vegetable oil	ton	938.00	Average price, 12.4.1 in Table C-9

TABLE C-6
Derivation of the Estimated Output in Table 12

	Unit	1949	1950	1951	1952	1953	1954	1955	1956	1957
1.1	Generating capacity, year-end	1000 Kw	1,849	1,866	1,883	1,964	2,350	2,597	2,997	3,611	4,635
1.2	Annual average capacity	1000 Kw	1,850	1,858	1,875	1,910	2,157	2,474	2,797	3,202	4,123
1.3	Utilization hours	hours	2,330	2,450	3,080	3,800	4,400	4,530	4,510	4,760	4,796
1.4	Estimated output of electricity	million Kwh	4,310	4,552	5,775	7,258	9,491	11,207	12,614	15,242	19,774
2.1	Total coal consumption in thermal plants, in natural units	1000 tons					4,854	5,310	6,525	8,364	
2.2	Total coal consumption converted into standard units	1000 tons					4,421	4,855	5,938	7,494	
2.3	Rate of standard coal consumption,	Kg/Kwh					.653	.639	.621	.594	

143

TABLE C-6 (*continued*)

	Unit	1949	1950	1951	1952	1953	1954	1955	1956	1957
2.4	Estimated output of thermal electricity	million Kwh				6,770	7,597	9,561	12,616	
3.1	Steel produced by open-hearth furnaces	1000 tons				1,110			3,210	3,884
3.2	Steel produced by electric furnaces	1000 tons				142			608	769
3.3	Steel produced by converters	1000 tons				135			647	783
3.4	Estimated total steel output	1000 tons				1,387			4,465	5,436
4.1	Total effective volume of blast furnaces, year-end	cubic meters				5,179	7,739	8,987	9,996	12,077	

TABLE C-6 (*continued*)

	Unit	1949	1950	1951	1952	1953	1954	1955	1956	1957
4.2 Estimated annual average effective volume	cubic meters					6,459	8,363	9,491	11,036	
4.3 Utilization coefficient of blast furnaces	tons/$m^3 \cdot$day					1.034	1.112	1.165	1.305	
4.4 Estimated output of pig iron	1000 tons					2,435	3,387	4,033	5,253	
5.1 Total effective base area of open-hearth furnaces, year-end	square meters							1,024.3	1,668.6	
5.2 Estimated annual average effective base area	square meters								1,346.4	
5.3 Utilization coefficient of open-hearth furnaces	tons/$m^2 \cdot$day								6.67	

TABLE C-6 (*continued*)

	Unit	1949	1950	1951	1952	1953	1954	1955	1956	1957
5.4 Estimated output of open-hearth steel	1000 tons								3,277	
6.1 Coke ratio for steel produced by open-hearth furnaces	Kg/ton				2.85				1.81	1.81
6.2 Steel output of open-hearth furnaces	1000 tons				1,110				3,210	3,884
6.3 Coke consumed in open-hearth furnaces	1000 tons				3.16				5.81	7.03
6.4 Coke ratio for steel produced by converters	kg/ton				150				144	144
6.5 Steel output of converters	1000 tons				135				647	783

146

TABLE C-6 (*continued*)

	Unit	1949	1950	1951	1952	1953	1954	1955	1956	1957
6.6 Coke consumed in converters	1000 tons				20.25				93.17	112.75
6.7 Coke ratio for blast furnaces	kg/ton				941				791	779
6.8 Output of pig iron	1000 tons				1,878				4,777	5,887
6.9 Coke consumed in blast furnaces	1000 tons				1,767.20				3,778.61	4,585.97
6.10 Estimated output of metallurgical coke	1000 tons				1,790				3,878	4,706
7.1 Electricity consumed per ton of coal	Kwh/ton				13.4			15.5	13.7	
7.2 Total electricity consumption in the coal industry	million Kwh				820			1,512	1,530	

TABLE C-6 (continued)

	Unit	1949	1950	1951	1952	1953	1954	1955	1956	1957
7.3 Estimated output of coal	1000 tons				61,194			97,540	111,670	
8.1 Domestic output of cotton	1000 tan = 50 tons	8,888	13,849	20,611	26,074	23,495	21,298	30,369	28,903	
8.2 Domestic cotton used for making yarns	1000 tan = 50 tons	5,725	8,920	13,276	16,794	15,133	13,718	19,561	18,616	
8.3 Import of cotton	1000 tan = 50 tons	1,033	2,678	1,226	1,536	219	839	1,727	882	
8.4 Total cotton used for making yarns	1000 tan = 50 tons		8,403	10,146	14,812	17,013	15,972	15,445	20,443	
8.5 Average consumption of cotton per bale of yarn	Kg/bale		201.84	200.64	198.97	196.50	195.36	192.62	194.83	
8.6 Estimated output of cotton yarn	1000 bales		2,082	2,528	3,722	4,329	4,088	4,009	5,246	

TABLE C-6 (*continued*)

	Unit	1949	1950	1951	1952	1953	1954	1955	1956	1957
9.1	Output of cotton yarns	1000 bales				3,620	4,100	4,600	3,970	5,246	
9.2	Cotton yarns used for making cloth	1000 bales				2,947	3,338	3,745	3,232	4,274	
9.3	Consumption of yarns per 1000 meters of cloth	Kg/1000m				137.31	134.53	136.28	133.70	134.58	
9.4	Estimated output of cotton cloth	million meters				3,893	4,505	4,987	4,385	5,760	
10.1	Number of spindles installed, year-end	1000	4,996	5,128	5,284	5,610	5,891	6,303	6,671	6,820	7,620
10.2	Estimated average number of spindles in the year	1000		5,062	5,206	5,447	5,751	6,097	6,487	6,746	7,220

149

TABLE C-6 (*continued*)

	Unit	1949	1950	1951	1952	1953	1954	1955	1956	1957
10.3 Rate of utilization of spindles	%		68.16	77.16	89.15	92.42	93.76	78.03	94.27	74.00
10.4 Estimated total number of spindle-hours	1000 spindle-hrs.		23,760	27,660	33,430	36,590	39,370	34,850	43,780	36,790
10.5 Output per 1000 spindle-hours	Kg		21.20	21.75	22.49	24.37	25.63	25.53	26.69	25.00
10.6 Estimated output of cotton yarns	1000 bales		2,776	3,315	4,143	4,914	5,561	4,903	6,440	5,069
11.1 Number of power looms installed, year-end	1000				142	151	164	169	175	
11.2 Estimated average number of power looms in the year	1000					147	158	167	172	

TABLE C-6 (*continued*)

	Unit	1949	1950	1951	1952	1953	1954	1955	1956	1957
11.3 Rate of utilization of looms	%					94.36	92.93	74.54	94.40	
11.4 Estimated total number of loom-hours	million loom-hours					955.0	1,010.9	857.1	1,117.9	
11.5 Output per loom-hour	meter					4.258	4.331	4.316	4.393	
11.6 Estimated output of cotton cloth produced by power looms	million meters					4,066	4,378	3,699	4,911	

151

Rate and Pattern of Industrial Growth in Communist China

Sources of Data in Table C-6:

1.1	For 1949-1956, from *CH*, pp. 46 and 64.
	For 1957, from *JMJP*, Oct. 11, 1959.
1.2	Arithmetic mean of two successive year-end figures in 1.1. For 1949, 1952, and 1956 actual figures are given in *CH*, pp. 50 and 68.
1.3	For 1949-1956, from *CH*, pp. 49 and 68.
	For 1957, from *TGY*, p. 108.
1.4	= (1.2) × (1.3).

2.1	*CH*, p. 62.
2.2	Figures in (2.1) are broken down into high-grade coal and low-grade coal (see *CH*, p. 62). High-grade coal is assumed to have a heat value of 7,000 Kcal per kg, based on the information given in *SLFT*, No. 4, 1958, p. 4; and low-grade coal is assumed to have a heat value of 5,000 Kcal per kg. Based on the information given in *SLFT*, No. 5, 1958, p. 4. Standard coal as defined by the Chinese Communists has 7,000 Kcal per kg.
2.3	*CH*, p. 69.
2.4	(2.2) ÷ (2.3).

3.1	For 1952 and 1956, calculated from data in *YCP*, No. 1, 1958, p. 35.
	For 1957, calculated from data in *YCP*, No. 4, 1958, p. 12.
3.2	For 1952 and 1956, from *CH*, p. 22.
	For 1957, calculated from data in *YCP*, No. 7, 1958, p. 38.
3.3	For 1952 and 1956, calculated from data in *YCP*, No. 1, 1958, p. 35.
	For 1957, calculated from data in *YCP*, No. 190, 1960, pp. 14-16.
3.4	= (3.1) + (3.2) + (3.3).

4.1	*CH*, p. 16.
4.2	Arithmetic mean of two successive year-end figures in (4.1).
4.3	*CH*, p. 25.
4.4	= (4.2) × (4.3) × 365, assuming that blast furnaces worked 365 days a year.

5.1	*CH*, p. 17.
5.2	Arithmetic mean of two successive year-end figures in (5.1).
5.3	*CH*, p. 25.
5.4	= (5.2) × (5.3) × 365, assuming that open-hearth furnaces worked 365 days a year.

6.1	*YCP*, No. 1, 1958, p. 34. 1953's figure is taken for 1952 and 1956's for 1957.
6.2	Same in (3.1).
6.3	= (6.1) × (6.2).
6.4	*TCKT*, No. 18, 1957, p. 33. 1953's figure is taken for 1952 and 1956's for 1957.
6.5	Same in (3.3).
6.6	= (6.4) × (6.5).
6.7	*TCKT*, No. 18, 1957, p. 33. 1953's figure is taken for 1952.
	For 1957, from *YCP*, No. 1, 1958, p. 8.
6.8	Table C-1.
6.9	= (6.7) × (6.8).
6.10	= (6.3) + (6.6) + (6.9).

7.1	*TCKT*, No. 18, 1957, p. 33. 1953's figure is taken for 1952.
7.2	*CH*, p. 72.

Statistical Data

Sources of Data in Table C-6 (*continued*)

7.3	$= (7.2) \div (7.1)$.

8.1 *CH*, p. 182.

8.2 $= (8.1) \times 0.6441$. The following information is given in *CH*, p. 189: The total quantity of cotton used in making yarns in 1956 was 20,443,000 tan, out of it, 882,000 tan was imported cotton in that year and 19,561,000 tan was domestic cotton cropped in 1955. The proportion of domestic cotton used in making yarns to total cotton output in 1955 was then:

$$\frac{19,561,000}{30,369,000} = 0.6441$$

8.3 *CH*, p. 182.

8.4 It is the sum of the figure of the preceding year in (8.2) plus the figure of the current year in (8.3).

8.5 For 1949, from *CH*, p. 157.
For 1952-1956, from *CH*, p. 170.
For 1950 and 1951, interpolated from the figures of 1949 and 1952.

8.6 $= (8.4) \div (8.5)$.

9.1 *TGY*, p. 99.

9.2 $= (9.1) \times 0.8141$. Cotton yarn used for making cloth in 1956 was given as 4,271,000 bales (*CH*, p. 190). Its ratio to the total cotton yarn output in 1956 is then

$$\frac{4,271,000}{5,246,000} = 0.8141$$

This ratio has been applied to all years in our calculations.

9.3 *CH*, p. 170.

9.4 $= (9.2) \div [(9.3) \div 181.44]$, where 181.44 is the weight in kg per bale of cotton yarn.

10.1 For 1949-1956, from *CH*, pp. 154, 162, and 194.
For 1957, from *HC*, No. 8, 1959, p. 2.

10.2 Arithmetic mean of two successive year-end figures in (10.1).

10.3 *CH*, pp. 155, 169 and 186.

10.4 Calculated from the following information:
1. The utilization rate of spindles is defined as (*KYTCH*, p. 378)

$$\frac{\text{Operating spindle hours}}{\text{Installed spindle hours}}$$

2. Installed spindle hours = 22.5 hours × statutory work days in a year × average number of installed spindles (*KYTCH*, p. 378).
3. There are 306 statutory work days in a year (*CKKY*, No. 7, 1956, p. 58).
4. So, for each year the total number of operating spindle hours = utilization rate × average number of installed spindles × 22.5 × 306.

10.5 For 1950-1956, from *CH*, pp. 157 and 170.
For 1957, from *CKFC*, No. 28, 1959, pp. 5-10.

10.6 $= (10.4) \times (10.5) \div 181.44$, where 181.44 is the weight in kg per bale of cotton yarn.

11.1 *CH*, pp. 154, 162, and 194.

153

Sources of Data in Table C-6 (*continued*)

11.2	Arithmetic mean of two successive year-end figures in (11.1).
11.3	*CH*, pp. 155 and 169.
11.4	$= (11.3) \times (11.2) \times 22.5 \times 306$. For explanations see (10.4).
11.5	*CH*, pp. 157 and 170.
11.6	$= (11.4) \times (11.5)$.

TABLE C-7

ANNUAL AVERAGE NUMBERS OF PRODUCTIVE WORKERS IN
INDIVIDUAL INDUSTRIES IN 1952

Industry	Number of Productive Workers
Electricity	29,700
Coal	318,000
Petroleum	13,250
Ferrous metal	134,415
Nonferrous metal	35,969
Metal processing	509,980
Machine building	248,360
Metal products and repairs	261,620
Chemical	72,550
Building materials	275,830
Timber	178,920
Textile	777,528
Paper	53,808
Food	468,410
Daily-use commodities	727,780
All industry	3,596,140

Sources of Data in Table C-7:

(1) The actual numbers of productive workers of the electric industry, the coal industry, the ferrous metal industry, the textile industry and the paper industry are given in *CH*, pp. 32, 67, 99, 174, and 211.

(2) As to the petroleum industry, the metal processing industry, the chemical industry, the building materials industry and the food industry, the number of productive workers in each industry is derived from the figure of total electric power consumption and the figure of power consumption per productive workers in that industry in 1952. All the power consumption figures are given in *CH*, pp. 72-73.

(3) In *TCKT*, No. 14, 1957, p. 30, it is reported that the production of timber per productive worker in the timber industry in 1952 was 56 cubic meters. It is already known that the total timber production excluding that of handicrafts was 10,020,000 cubic meters in 1952 (see *FFYP*, p. 37). This makes the total number of productive workers of that industry in 1952, 178,920.

(4) The figure of productive workers in the daily-use commodities industry is calculated from the following information:

(a) The total number of workers and other employees of the paper industry, the food industry and the daily-use commodities industry rose from 2,000,000 in 1952 to 2,850,000 in 1957. (See CKCKY, No. 18, 1959, p. 3.)

(b) The actual ratio of productive workers to total employment in these industries was 62.5%. (See *CKCKY*, No. 18, 1957, pp. 4-5.) This

Sources of Data in Table C-7 (*continued*)

means that the number of productive workers of these three industries in 1952 was 2,000,000 × .625 = 1,250,000.

(c) The figures of productive workers of the food industry and the paper industry in 1952 are known to be 468,410 and 53,807 respectively. So the number of productive workers in the daily-use commodities industry in that year is 1,250,000 — 468,410 — 53,808 = 727,782.

(5) The number of productive workers of the nonferrous metal industry in 1952 is simply a residue. The total number of productive workers of all industries except the electric industry can be calculated from the power consumption figures (*CH*, pp. 72-73), and it is 3,566,440. By subtracting the known figures of the other 11 industries, we obtained a residue of 35,967, which should be the number of productive workers of nonferrous metal in 1952.

(6) The number of productive workers in the metal processing industry is subdivided into that of machine building and that of metal products and repairs. It is stated on p. 129 of *CH* that the total workers and other employees of private machine building enterprises in 1955 was 92,653 which constituted 19.8% of total workers and employees of the machine building industry in the whole economy in that year. Thus the latter figure was 467,944. On the same page of *CH*, the figure of total workers and other employees of the metal processing industry in 1955 is given as 960,477. So the employment of the machine building was 48.71% of the total employment of the metal processing industry while that of metal products and repairs was 51.29%. This ratio is used to obtain the distribution of productive workers in the metal processing industry in 1952.

TABLE C-8
DISTRIBUTION OF WAGE BILL, 1952

Industry	Average Annual Wage Rate	Number of Productive Workers	Wage Bill (1,000 yuan)	Weight (%)
Electric	810.0	29,700	24,057	1.27
Coal	604.8	318,000	129,326	10.14
Petroleum	492.6	13,250	6,527	0.34
Ferrous metal	597.7	134,415	80,340	4.24
Nonferrous metal	478.3	35,969	17,204	0.91
Metal processing	586.0	509,980	298,848	15.76
Machine building		248,360	145,539	7.68
Metal products & repairs		261,620	153,309	8.08
Chemical	534.2	72,550	38,759	2.04
Building materials	470.9	275,830	129,888	6.85
Timber	525.0	178,920	93,933	4.95
Textile	553.0	777,528	429,973	22.67
Paper	503.3	53,808	27,082	1.43
Food	423.8	468,410	198,512	10.47
Daily-use commodities	493.0	727,780	358,796	18.92
All industry	527.3	3,596,140	1,896,245	100.00

Sources of Wage Rate Data:

(1) For the electric industry, the ferrous metal industry, the metal processing industry, the textile industry and the paper industry, wage rates are taken from *CH*, pp. 32, 52, 129, 175, and 212.

Rate and Pattern of Industrial Growth in Communist China

Sources of Wage Rate Data (continued)

---

(2) For the coal industry, see MTKY, No. 20, 1959, p. 23.

(3) For the timber industry, see TCKT, No. 14, 1957, p. 30.

(4) The national average wage rate of all industry is derived from the following information:

The average annual wage of industrial workers in 1955 was 599.6 yuan (see JPRS 3088, 1960, p. 4). The national average annual wage of industrial workers increased by 13.7% from 1952 to 1955 (see LT, No. 5, 1956, p. 3).

(5) For the petroleum industry, the nonferrous metal industry, the building materials industry, the food industry and the daily-use commodities industry, the average annual wage rates are calculated in the following steps:

(a) The average wage rates of these industries in 1956 can be calculated on the basis of the following information:

	Petroleum Industry	Nonferrous Metal Industry	Building Materials Industry	Food Industry	Daily-use Commodities Industry
Monthly wage of the 1st grade worker (yuan)	33.75	34.50	33.50	28.50	32.00
Monthly wage of the 8th grade worker (yuan)	105.60	110.40	99.00	71.30	90.70
Wage coefficient	3.13	3.20	3.00	2.50	2.78
Grade differential	17.7%	18.1%	16.8%	14.1%	15.7%
Average grade of workers in the industry	3.7	3.7	3.6	3.9	3.9

(See LT, No. 8, 1957, p. 26; TCKTTH, No. 23, 1956; CKCKY, No. 16, 1957, pp. 21-22; and LT, No. 7, 1957, p. 33.)

The so-called "grade differential" is the percentage increment in wage a worker gets when he is promoted by one grade. With these figures we can calculate the wage rates of the "average grades of workers" in the industries listed above. So the average monthly wage rates of these industries in 1956 are 52.54, 54.21, 50.31, 41.81 and 48.64 respectively.

(b) The 1956 wage rate of the nonferrous metal industry is converted into that of 1952 according to the index of wage rate increase in that industry as given in Chung Kung Yeh Kung Hui Tung Hsun (Bulletin of the Heavy Industry Labor Union) No. 3, 1957, p. 1. The rate of increase in wage rate of the paper industry (CH, p. 212) is used to convert the wage rates of the food industry and the daily-use commodities industry, while the rate of increase in wage rate of the metal processing industry (CH, p. 129) is used to convert the wage rates of the petroleum industry and the building materials industry.

(6) The only industry for which the average wage rate is not known is the chemical industry. By subtracting the wage bills, i.e. the products of wage rates times the number of workers, of the other 12 industries from the total wage bill of all industry, a residue is obtained. This is the wage bill of the chemical industry and it, after being divided by the number of workers of the chemical industry, yields an average wage rate for that industry of 534.2 yuan.

TABLE C-9
PRICE DATA
(in yuan)

Code Number	Commodity	Unit	Lowest Price	Highest Price	Number of Prices	Unweighted Average	Weighted Average
4.1.1	Steel Ingots	Ton	380.00	3000.00	118		656.35
4.2	Rolled Steel	Ton	570.00	13000.00	144		815.48
4.3.1	Pig Iron	Ton	135.00	297.35	10	199.29	
4.5	Manganese	Ton	84.00	328.00	24	218.33	
4.6.1	Metallurgical Coke	Ton	24.00	78.00	8	43.27	
6.1	Metal Cutting Machines	Ton			1	2703.00	
6.2.1	Internal Combustion	HP			3	332.60	
6.5	Electric Motors	KW			34	155.85	
6.6	A.C. Generators	KW			2	945.45	
6.9	Locomotives	Unit				257300.00	
6.10	R.R. Freight Cars	Unit				21480.00	
6.17	Plows	Set			1	78.10	
6.18	Ball Bearings	Set	7.00	40.00	7	19.71	
6.19	Transformers	KVA			42	36.86	
6.20	Merchant Vessels	Dwt					3323.00
6.22	Spindles	Unit			1	364.00	
6.23	Looms	Set			1	1550.00	
6.27	Bicycles	Unit	125.00	160.00	6	147.16	
6.28	Adding Machines	Set			1	270.00	
6.29	Typewriters	Set			1	70.00	
6.30	Sewing Machines	Set			1	190.00	
6.31	Radios	Set			1	77.00	
6.32	Clocks	Set			2	23.00	
7.1	Ammonium Sulphate	Ton	336.00	465.00	8	369.37	

TABLE C-9—Continued

Code Number	Commodity	Unit	Lowest Price	Highest Price	Number of Prices	Unweighted Average	Weighted Average
7.2	Ammonium Nitrate	Ton	235.00	489.00	1	2500.00	
7.4	Sulphuric Acid	Ton	352.50	383.75	10	398.90	
7.5	Soda Ash	Ton	820.00	1450.00	8	370.12	
7.6	Caustic Soda	Ton	433.00	461.00	15	1064.00	
7.8	Tires	Ton			4	440.00	
7.9	Penicillin	Kg.	10333.00	10833.00	2	10583.00	
7.10	Insecticide	Ton	120.00	130.00	2	125.00	
8.1	Cement	Ton	51.13	100.00	21	75.44	
8.2	Plain Glass	M²	1.61	7.70	9	3.13	
8.3	Asbestos	Ton	2000.00	4500.00	4	3250.00	
10.1	Cotton Yarn	Bale	525.00	1275.00	49		860.70
10.2.1	Cotton Cloth	Meter	0.60	1.75	174		0.85
10.3	Gunny Sacks	Piece	0.90	3.30	9	2.27	
10.4	Woolen Fabrics	Meter	4.95	15.15	10	8.54	
10.5	Woolen Yarn	Kg.	22.04	44.09	13	33.95	
10.6	Woolen Blankets	Piece			1	118.00	
10.7	Domesticated Silk	Ton	30400.00	55800.00	6	47066.00	
10.8	Tassah Silk	Ton			1	22000.00	
10.9.1	Silk Fabrics	Meter	3.20	9.18	5	5.46	
10.10	Cotton Undervest	Dozen			1	5.80	
10.11	Socks	Dozen	4.67	10.80	16		7.10
10.12	Cotton Dress and Pants	Dozen	29.70	30.67	8	29.94	
10.13	Cotton Underwear	Dozen	40.51	40.51	6	40.51	
10.14	Towels	Dozen	4.53	9.87	12	8.56	
11.1.1.1	Newsprint	Ton	1000.00	3023.00	11	1870.00	
11.1.1.2	Cigarette Paper	Ton			1	6550.00	
11.1.1.3	Cardboard	Ton			1	240.00	

TABLE C-9—*Continued*

Code Number	Commodity	Unit	Lowest Price	Highest Price	Number of Prices	Unweighted Average	Weighted Average
12.1.1	Sugar	Ton	840.00	1570.00	51	1265.00	
12.2.1	Salt	Ton	183.00	274.00	21	235.00	
12.3	Cigarettes	Crate	363.00	1440.00	63	685.00	
12.4.1	Edible Vegetable Oil	Ton	740.00	1160.00	45	938.00	
12.5	Flour	Ton	205.00	390.00	72	346.00	
12.6	Alcoholic Beverages	Ton	860.00	1794.00	11	1376.00	
12.7	Alcohol	Ton	1780.00	2200.00	2	2000.00	
12.9	Dairy Products	Ton	4000.00	8800.00	11	6570.00	
12.12	Soap	Ton	642.00	1177.50	28	976.50	
13.1	Rubber Footwear	Pair	1.75	14.44	38	4.44	
13.2	Matches	Crate	11.76	21.90	16	18.43	
13.3	Light Leather	M²	5.40	16.50	6	11.10	
13.4	Heavy Leather	Ton	1200.00	9240.00	11	3851.00	
13.6	Enamel Cups	Unit	0.48	0.80	2	0.64	
13.7	Enamel Wash-basins	Unit	4.00	6.50	3	4.90	
13.8	Pencils	Dozen	0.72	1.51	6	1.02	
13.9	Fountain Pens	Unit	3.08	6.27	15	4.75	
13.10	Thermos bottles	Unit	1.50	1.50	2	1.50	
13.12	Accordians	Unit			1	171.00	

Rate and Pattern of Industrial Growth in Communist China

Sources of the Price Data in Table C-9:

4.1.1	Price Data are from *KYCT*, Jan. 1952. For classification of quality steel and ordinary steel, see *The Concise Scientific and Technic Dictionary*, Shanghai, p. 116; and *Brief Explanations of Popular Industrial Terms and Technology*. Science Promotion Publishing Company, 1958, Peking, p. 48.
	The proportions of quality steel and ordinary steel in the total output of steel ingots in 1952 are given in *CH*, p. 22.
4.2	Price Data are from *KYCT*, Jan. 1952. The proportions of quality steel ingots and ordinary steel ingots are used in deriving the weighted average price of rolled steel.
4.3.1	from *KYCT*, Jan. 1952.
4.5	*KYCT*, Jan. 1952.
4.6.1	*TTJP*, Jan. 1, 1952, and *CFJP*, Jan. 1, 1952.
6.1	It is stated (*CHCC*, No. 9, 1957, pp. 11-15) that 3.7 tons of ferrous metals is used per 10,000 yuan's worth of metal cutting machines. We assume that metal cutting machines are made entirely of ferrous metals.
6.2.1	*KYCT*, Jan. 1952.
6.5	*KYCT*, Jan. 1952.
6.6	*KYCT*, Jan. 1952.
6.9	Derived from the information of production costs and profits of two locomotive plants in 1957 and the industrial price index of 1957/1952. See *CCKY*, No. 6, 1958, p. 9, and *TGY*, p. 87.
6.10	Derived in the same way as locomotives with information furnished by the same sources.
6.17	The price of double wheel and double blade plows quoted in *Nan Fang Jih Pao* (The Southern Daily), June 17, 1956, deflated by the price index of industrial equipment, given in *HP*, p. 459.
6.18	*KYCT*, Jan. 1952.
6.19	*KYCT*, Jan. 1952.
6.20	Derived in the following steps:
	(1) Total gross value of production of the machine building industry in 1956 was 5760 million yuan. (See *CH*, p. 121.)
	(2) The total value of merchant vessels produced in 1956 was 6% of the gross value of production of the whole machine building industry (see *HCKTKY*, p. 43), so the total value of merchant vessels was 345.6 million yuan in 1956.
	(3) The total tonnage of merchant vessels produced in 1956 was 104,000 dwt tons, so it was 3,323 yuan per dwt ton.
	(4) No deflating is needed to get the 1952's price per dwt ton of merchant vessels because the total gross value in 1956 was calculated according to 1952's constant prices.
6.22	According to Kao Kang's report, 655,200,000 yuan could buy 1,800,000 new spindles at the 1951 end-of-the-year price, so the unit price should be 364 yuan. (See *CCCP*, No. 43, 1953, p. 43.)
6.23	*KYCT*, Jan. 1952.
6.27	*KYCT*, Jan. 1952.
6.28	*KYCT*, Jan. 1952.
6.29	*Directory of Northern China Urban-Rural Commodities Interflow Exhibition*, No. 16, p. 40.
6.30	*TCKT*, No. 4, 1957, p. 6.
6.31	*NCNA*, Feb. 9, 1961, English.

Sources of the Price Data in Table C-9 (*continued*)

6.32	*JMJP*, July 19, 1956. They are 1956 prices and have to be converted into 1952 prices by using the industrial equipment price index of 1956/1952 (*HP*, p. 459) as the deflator.
7.1	*CFJP*, Jan. 1, 1952 and *TTJP*, Jan. 1, 1952.
7.2	*KYCT*, Jan. 1952.
7.4	*KYCT*, Jan. 1952.
7.5	*CFJP*, Jan. 1, 1952 and *TTJP*, Jan. 1, 1952.
7.6	*KYCT*, Jan. 1952.
7.8	*KYCT*, Jan. 1952.
7.9	*CFJP*, Jan. 1, 1952.
7.10	*CFJP*, July 20, 1952, deflated into January's price by using the price index given in *HP*, p. 457.
8.1	*KYCT*, Jan. 1952.
8.2	*KYCT*, Jan. 1952.
8.3	*KYCT*, Jan. 1952.
10.1	*CFJP*, Jan. 1, 1952 and *TTJP*, Jan. 1, 1952. The weighted average price is derived according to the following proportions:

High count yarn (over 28 counts)	20%
Low count yarn (below 20 counts)	10%
Medium count yarn (20-28 counts)	70%
(See *JPRS*, 756, 1958)	

10.2.1	Prices are from *CFJP*, Jan. 1, 1952 and *TTJP*, Jan. 1, 1952. The average prices are weighted by the following ratios:

	Quantity	Average Price	Weight
white cloth	1955 million meters	0.76/meter	51%
colored cloth	1875 million meters	0.94/meter	49%

(See the output data)

10.3	*CFJP*, Jan. 1952 and *TTJP*, Jan. 1, 1952.
10.4	*CFJP*, Jan. 1952 and *TTJP*, Jan. 1, 1952.
10.5	*CFJP*, Jan. 1, 1952 and *TTJP*, Jan. 1, 1952.
10.6	*Ta Kung Pao*, Chungking, Dec. 30, 1951.
10.7	*CFJP*, Jan. 1, 1952.
10.8	*CFJP*, Jan. 1, 1952.
10.9.1	*CFJP*, Jan. 1, 1952.
10.10	*Directory of Northern China Urban-Rural Commodities Interflow Exhibition*, No. 13, p. 35.
10.11	*CFJP*, Jan. 1, 1952 and *TTJP*, Jan. 1, 1952.
10.12	*CFJP*, Jan. 1, 1952 and *TTJP*, Jan. 1, 1952.
10.13	*CFJP*, Jan. 1, 1952.
10.14	*CFJP*, Jan. 1, 1952 and *TTJP*, Jan. 1, 1952.
11.1.1.1	*CFJP*, Jan. 1, 1952 and *TTJP*, Jan. 1, 1952.
11.1.1.2	*Ta Kung Pao*, Chungking, Dec. 30, 1951.
11.1.1.3	*CFJP*, Jan. 1, 1952.
12.1.1	*CFJP*, Jan. 1, 1952 and *TTJP*, Jan. 1, 1952.
12.2.1	*CFJP*, Jan. 1, 1952 and *TTJP*, Jan. 1, 1952.
12.3	*CFJP*, Jan. 1, 1952 and *TTJP*, Jan. 1, 1952.
12.4.1	*CFJP*, Jan. 1, 1952 and *TTJP*, Jan. 1, 1952.
12.5	*CFJP*, Jan. 1, 1952 and *TTJP*, Jan. 1, 1952.

Sources of the Price Data in Table C-9 (*continued*)

12.6	*Compilation of Nankai Index Materials,* Nankai University, 1958, Peking, p. 202; and *Hsin Win Jih Pao,* Shanghai, Nov. 19, 1952.
12.7	*Compilation of Nankai Index Materials,* p. 245.
12.9	*CFJP,* Jan. 1, 1952.
12.12	*CFJP,* Jan. 1, 1952 and *TTJP,* Jan. 1, 1952.
13.1	*CFJP,* Jan. 1, 1952 and *TTJP,* Jan. 1, 1952.
13.2	*CFJP,* Jan. 1, 1952 and *TTJP,* Jan. 1, 1952.
13.3	*CFJP,* Jan. 1, 1952 and *TTJP,* Jan. 1, 1952.
13.4	*CFJP,* Jan. 1, 1952 and *TTJP,* Jan. 1, 1952.
13.6	*Ta Kung Pao,* Chungking, Dec. 30, 1952.
13.7	*Ta Kung Pao,* Chungking, Dec. 30, 1952.
13.8	*CFJP,* Jan. 1, 1952.
13.9	*CFJP,* Jan. 1, 1952.
13.10	*TTJP,* Jan. 1, 1952 and *Ta Kung Pao,* Chungking, Dec. 30, 1951.
13.12	*Chungking Jih Pao,* July 25, 1956, deflated into 1952's price.

Notes

NOTES TO CHAPTER I

1. As to a detailed discussion of the concept and the coverage of "basic construction investment" in Communist China, readers are referred to Choh-Min Li, *Economic Development of Communist China*, University of California Press, 1959, Berkeley and Los Angeles, pp. 112-7.

2. For instance, *op. cit.*, pp. 35-7.

NOTES TO CHAPTER II

1. It is an average of changes in physical output of individual commodities. However, it may be taken, with certain qualifications, to measure economic welfare or productive potential for an economy. See J. R. Hicks, "The Valuation of the Social Income," *Economica*, N.S. VII (May 1940), pp. 105-24; S. Kuznets, "On the Valuation of Social Income—Reflections on Professor Hicks' Article," *Economica*, N.S. XV (Feb. and May 1948), pp. 1-16 and pp. 116-131; I. M. D. Little, "The Valuation of Social Income," *Economica*, N.S. XVI (Feb. 1949), pp. 11-26; P. A. Samuelson, "Evaluation of Real National Income," *Oxford Economic Papers*, N.S. Vol. 2 (Jan. 1950), pp. 1-29; G. Warren Nutter, "On Measuring Economic Growth," *Journal of Political Economy*, LXV (Feb. 1957), pp. 51-63; and R. H. Moorsteen, "On Measuring Productive Potential and Relative Efficiency," *Quarterly Journal of Economics*, LXXV (Aug. 1961), pp. 451-467.

2. In case of data deficiencies other indicators, such as deliveries of goods or labor time used, may be taken as approximations to the output series.

3. See the United Nations Statistical Office, "Index Numbers of Industrial Production," *Studies in Methods*, No. 1, 1950, p. 21; S. Fabricant, *The Output of Manufacturing Industries, 1890-1937*,

National Bureau of Economic Research, 1940, New York, p. 25; and R. C. Geary, "The Concept of the Net Volume of Output with Special Reference to Irish Data," *Journal of the Royal Statistical Society*, Vol. CVII, Parts III-IV, 1944.

4. If a base-weights (Laspeyres type) formula or another fixed-weights formula is chosen, the weighting period would be either the base period or any other given period. If a current-weights (Paasche type) formula is chosen, the weights have to be taken from the period which is to be compared with the base period.

5. See "Revised Federal Reserve Monthly Index of Industrial Production," *Federal Reserve Bulletin*, Dec. 1953, p. 1278; and the United Nations Statistical Office, *op. cit.*, p. 6.

6. The United Nations Statistical Office, *op. cit.*, p. 6; *Federal Reserve Bulletin*, Dec. 1953, *ibid.*; and F. C. Mills, *Statistical Method*, 3rd edition, Henry Holt & Co., 1955, New York, p. 490.

7. The United Nations Statistical Office, *op. cit.*, pp. 54 and 57-59; *Federal Reserve Bulletin*, Dec. 1953, *ibid.*; and F. C. Mills, *op. cit.*, pp. 505-506.

8. For instance, this weighting system has been used in constructing output indexes for Soviet Russia. See D. R. Hodgman, *Soviet Industrial Production, 1928-1951*, Harvard University Press, 1954, and N. M. Kaplan and R. H. Moorsteen, *Indexes of Soviet Industrial Output*, RM-2495, the RAND Corporation, May 13, 1960.

9. There are some newly invented index formulae. See, for instance, G. Stuvel, "A New Index Number Formula," *Econometrica*, Vol. 25, No. 1, Jan. 1957, pp. 123-131; K. S. Banerjee, "A Generalization on Stuvel's Index Number Formulae," *Econometrica*, Vol. 27, No. 4, Oct. 1959, pp. 676-678; and H. Theil, "Best Linear Index Numbers of Prices and Quantities," *Econometrica*, Vol. 28, No. 2, April 1960, pp. 464-480. Stuvel's new index formula should be classified as a modified current-weights formula because V_N in his formula is nothing but Σpq of the given year.

NOTES TO CHAPTER III

1. *The Ten Great Years*, hereafter referred to as *TGY*, is the most comprehensive statistical handbook ever made available to the public by the Chinese Communist authorities. There is both a Chinese version and an English version. All page numbers of this book quoted in this study are from the English version published by Foreign Languages Press, Peking, 1960.

2. "Factory-reporting method" is a literal translation of "kung-chang-chi-suan-fa," but individual factories may not be the reporting

units. According to the official definition, a reporting unit is a production establishment which satisfies the following conditions:

(a) It has its own independent accounting system, including an independent balance sheet of assets and liabilities and an independent profit and loss statement.

(b) It has the right to sign contracts with other enterprises.

(c) It has an independent account with state banks. See SSB, "Several Problems to be Noted in Regard to the Statistical Work of 1957's Annual Industrial Reports," *TCK T*, 1957, No. 23, p. 15; and Tsou I-jen, *Compilation of Statistical Terminology and Formulae*, revised ed., The New Knowledge Publishing Co., 1957, Shanghai, p. 30.

3. Articles and writings of Communist economists in Mainland China on this topic are numerous. The important ones are: Sun Yeh-fang, "On Gross Production Value and Related Problems," *TCK T*, No. 13, July 1957, pp. 8-14, and three articles following it in the same issue; "Materials on Methods of Computing the Gross Value of Industrial Product," *TCKTTH*, No. 17, Sept. 1956, pp. 2-5; "Several Problems of Computing the Gross Value of Industrial Product," *TCKTTH*, No. 17, Sept. 1956, pp. 1-2; "Diverse Opinions on the Methods of Computing the Gross Value of Industrial Product," *TCKTTH*, No. 24, Dec. 1956, pp. 5-10; and Yueh Wei, "The Method of Computing National Income," *CCYC*, No. 3, Aug. 1956, pp. 48-66.

4. For instance, Anshan Iron and Steel Works is allowed to count twice the value of pig iron produced by itself and used up in making steel in the calculation of the gross value of production. See the provisions for computing gross value given in *TCKTTH*, No. 11, June 1956, pp. 30-32.

5. This source has been quoted by a magazine published in Hong Kong. See Chao I-nung, "The Industry of Communist China in 1958," *China Weekly*, June 1, 1959, pp. 18-20. The same article has also quoted some other interesting figures from the Communist sources. They are: 47,963 agricultural tool manufacturing plants were established by the county governments and the people's communes in 1958; 150,000 factories were formed by 21,000 schools in the same year.

6. See *TCKTTH*, No. 11, June 1956, p. 32.

7. Lo Chin-hua, "A Problem of Using Gross Value to Check the Production Plan in the Local Machinery Industries," *TCKT*, No. 4, Feb. 1957, pp. 5-8.

8. Sun Yeh-fang, *op. cit.*, p. 9.

9. *Ibid.*, p. 10.

10. "A Study on the Gross Value of Output and the Net Value of Output," *TCYC*, No. 2, 1958, p. 28.

11. Ku Wei-lin and Chu Cheng-kang, "Problems Regarding the Gross Value of Production in the Chemical Industry," *HHKY*, No. 15, Aug. 1959, pp. 35-36.

12. See Lo Keng-mo, "A Study on the Problems of Profits in Prices and the Rate of Profit," *CHCC*, No. 1, 1956, and his "Problems of the Turnover Tax on Products of Heavy Industries," *CCYC*, No. 3, 1956, pp. 26-32; Fan Jo-i, "A Discussion on the Problems of Lowering the Internal Transfer Prices of the Means of Production," *CHCC*, No. 2, 1956, and his "Further Remarks on the Price Policy of the Heavy Industry's Products," *CCYC*, No. 3, 1957, pp. 54-67; Nan Ping and Suo Chen, "On the Price Problem of the Means of Production," *CCYC*, No. 2, 1957, pp. 12-24; and Fan Jo-i, "Price Policy and the Law of Value," *CCYC*, No. 5, 1958, pp. 45-49.

13. Fan Jo-i, "Further Remarks on the Price Policy of the Heavy Industry's Products," *CCYC*, No. 4, 1957, pp. 54 and 62. This means that the original profit-cost ratio was more than 210%. In Communist China as well as in Soviet Russia the profitability of a firm is indicated by its profit-cost ratio which is equivalent to what is known as "profit mark-up" in business circles in Western countries. We know, of course, that the earning power of a firm is more properly measured by its profit-capital ratio than by profit-cost ratio. However, information about the former ratio is not available in most cases.

14. The reduction in prices of producers' goods, mainly the ferrous metallurgical products and machinery, in 1956 had reduced the gross receipts of heavy industries in that year by 1.7 billion yuan. See Lo Keng-mo, *Problems of Commodity and Value under the Socialist System*, Science Publishing Company, 1957, Peking, p. 55.

15. In *TGY*, p. 87, gross output of the whole industrial sector in 1957 valued at 1957 constant prices is given as 70,400 million yuan while the output of the same year valued at 1952 constant prices is 78,390 million yuan. The ratio of these two figures, which is 89.8% is exactly a weighted price index with 1957 quantities as weights, i.e. $\Sigma p_{57}q_{57}/\Sigma p_{52}q_{57}$. The price ratios for producers' goods and consumers' goods are calculated in the same way.

16. SSB, Department of Industry, "Explanations of Certain Problems Arising from the Computation of 1957 Constant Prices for Industrial Products," *TCKT*, No. 9, Oct. 1957, pp. 11-13.

17. Hsu I, "Several Problems Concerning the Economic Accounting," *CCYC*, No. 4, 1958, p. 71.

18. For instance, the production of penicillin had increased 157,800 times in the short period of six years. See *TGY*, p. 97.

19. Ku Wei-lin and Chu Cheng-kang, *op. cit.*, p. 35.

20. A thorough discussion of all possible deficiencies in this connection can be found in Yin Ta-jen, "Several Methods of Computing the Production Values of Private Industries on the Basis of Constant Prices," *TCKTTH*, No. 11, 1955, pp. 37-40. Also see the *Survey and Statistics of the Private Industries in China During the Transitional Period*, edited by SSB, Department of Industry, Statistical Publishing Company, 1958, Peking, pp. 20-41.

21. See *TGY*, pp. 87, 88, and 91.

22. This has been translated also as "marine products" or "fishery."

23. Speech given by Hsu Teh-hang before the fourth meeting of the First National People's Congress, July 5, 1957, collected in the *Collection of Materials of the Fourth Meeting of the First National People's Congress of the People's Republic of China*, People's Publishing Company, 1957, Peking, pp. 430-438.

24. *Ibid.*

25. *Ibid.*

26. See *FFYP*, p. 89; *Brief Explanations on Terms of the First Five Year Plan for National Economic Development of the People's Republic of China*, People's Publishing Company, 1955, Peking, p. 31; SSB, *Communique for 1955* and *Communique for 1956*.

27. See *TGY*, p. 100. It is interesting to note that in a Russian book, published in 1959, on the economic development of Communist China based on official Chinese sources, aquatic outputs were still classified as agricultural products. The output figures for aquatic products for years from 1949 to 1958 given in this book are identical to those in *TGY*. See Yu. N. Kapelinskiy, L. A. Kisvyantsw, M. S. Pankin, Yu. A. Nekshev, V. P. Senin, and V. G. Sychev, *Development of the Economy and Foreign Economic Contacts of the People's Republic of China*, translated by U.S. Joint Publications Research Service (JPRS) 3234, May 23, 1960, p. 321.

28. Employment was estimated to be about 60,000 in 1959. See Hsu Teh-hang, "A New Situation of Sustained Leap Forward Has Developed in the Aquatic Enterprises," *JMJP*, April 7, 1960.

29. See *FFYP*, pp. 37, 60, and 61.

30. The statistical designations and coverages actually used by the local offices which conduct the surveys vary seriously from locality to locality. Moreover, most figures are merely rough estimates. For details of the surveys, see *Materials of the National Survey on the Handicraft Industry in 1954*, edited by the Division of Handicraft Industry, the Institute of Economic Research, Academy of Science, San Lien Book Company, 1957, Peking.

31. Teng Chieh, *A Preliminary Evaluation of the Socialist Transformation of China's Handicraft Industries*, People's Publishing Company, 1958, Peking, p. 101.

NOTES TO CHAPTER IV

1. The reliance on physical output series also has its own disadvantages such as (1) the necessarily limited sample, (2) the difficulty in handling new commodities and quality changes, and (3) the change over time in the relative importance of the sample. Some of the shortcomings will be discussed in greater detail in Section 1, Chapter V.

2. See D. B. Shimkin, *Minerals—A Key to Soviet Power*, Harvard University Press, 1953, p. 320; J. H. Blackman, "Transportation" in A. Bergson (ed.) *Soviet Economic Growth*, Row Peterson & Company, 1953, p. 128; and F. Seton, "The Tempo of Soviet Industrial Expansion," *Manchester Statistical Society*, January 9, 1957.

3. *Weekly Report* of the German Institute for Business Research, Berlin, April 30, 1940, p. 44.

4. G. Warren Nutter, "Industrial Growth in the Soviet Union," *American Economic Review*, Vol. XLVIV, May 1958, p. 402.

5. Colin Clark, *The Conditions of Economic Progress*, 2nd ed., MacMillan & Co., 1951, London, pp. 163-192.

6. Alexander Gerschenkron, *A Dollar Index of Soviet Machinery Output, 1927-28 to 1937*, R-197, April 6, 1951. The RAND Corporation; and *Economic Backwardness in Historical Perspective*, Harvard University Press, 1962, pp. 235-53.

7. Donald R. Hodgman, *Soviet Industrial Production, 1928-1951*, Harvard University Press, 1954.

8. Franklyn D. Holzman, *Soviet Taxation*, Harvard University Press, 1955, p. 5.

9. "Revised Federal Reserve Monthly Index of Industrial Production," *Federal Reserve Bulletin,* Dec. 1953, p. 1272. This has not been changed in the 1959 revision. See Board of Governors of the Federal Reserve System, *Industrial Production, 1959 Revision,* 1960, Washington, D.C.

10. Concrete examples given by Communist writers are the substitutions actually taking place and the relative price problems between gasoline and diesel oil, between gasoline and kerosene, among various kinds of timber used as building materials, and among various kinds of chemical fertilizers. See Nan Ping & Suo Chen, "On the Price Problem of the Means of Production," *CCYC,* No. 2, 1957, p. 15, and their "Value of the Means of Production and the Function of the Law of Value under Socialist System," *CCYC,* No. 1, 1957, pp. 50-51; Lo Keng-mo, "Problems of the Turnover Tax on Products of Heavy Industries," *CCYC,* No. 3, 1956, p. 31, and Fan Jo-i, "Further Remarks on the Price Policy of the Heavy Industry's Products," *CCYC,* No. 3, 1957, p. 65.

11. Wei Chiang, "The Transition from Capitalist Economy to State-Capitalist Economy," *CCYC,* No. 2, 1956, p. 64.

12. The signal of the "Five-Anti" campaign was first given by Chou En-lai in his speech delivered to the Standing Committee of the National Committee of the PPCC on January 5, 1952. During this campaign more than 450,000 private firms in nine big cities were investigated. More than 340,000 of them were found guilty of various "crimes," hence punished with penalties ranging from fine to confiscation. See *CN,* p. 23.

13. The official functions of the Ministry of Labor were the following:

    (a) Framing labor legislation.
    (b) Enforcing, or supervising the enforcement of, the labor laws.
    (c) Mediating disputes between workers and private employers.
    (d) Being in charge of the relief and placement of unemployed workers.

    However, it was said by Li Li-san, then Minister of Labor, that mediating labor disputes became the "sole" work of the local agencies of the Ministry of Labor in the early years of that regime. See Li Li-san's "Report on the Labor Policies and the Functions of the Ministry of Labor," in *The Compilation of Economic and Financial Policies and Regulations of the Central Government,* Vol. 1, 1950, Peking, pp. 676-78.

14. Hsing Yu-hung, "Several Important Works in Allocating Labor Force at the Present Time," *JMJP*, Aug. 14, 1955; also the editorial of *JMJP*, "Strengthening the Works of Allocating Labor Force and Avoiding the Waste of Labor," *JMJP*, July 17, 1955.

15. Yang I, "Rearranging the Labor Organizations in the State Enterprises of Coal Mine," *HHYP*, No. 9, 1954, p. 147; also *HHYP*, 1953, No. 5, p. 177.

16. See Articles 1, 4 and 5 of Chapter 1 in the Outline of Labor Regulations for State-Operated Enterprises, *People's Handbook*, 1955, p. 352.

17. *JMJP*, Aug. 14, 1955.

18. *JMJP*, Dec. 14, 1957.

19. See Wu Pin-chia, "The Wage System in the Lushun-Daren Area," *CKKY*, 1950, No. 6, p. 11; The Ministry of Industry, Northeastern People's Government, "Decree on the Wage Rates and the Eight-Grade Wage System," *CCCP*, Aug. 23, 1951, pp. 145-47.

20. The "equalitarianism" idea meant that all workers should be paid similarly regardless of the type of work or their skills; the "principle of using wages as a means of relief" meant that wage differentials should be determined by a worker's number of dependents instead of by the type of work he performed.

21. See, for example, Sung Chia-pu and Chou Heng-liu "How To Carry Out the Piece-Rate Wage System," *CKKY*, 1952, No. 9, p. 37, and "To Establish and Improve the Bonus System," *JMJP*, May 3, 1956.

22. Employment data are given by *FFYP*, pp. 128-29, as follows:

	Industry	Commerce	Industry and Commerce
Total employment	5,406,000	3,454,000	8,860,000
Employment in private sector	2,542,000	2,320,000	4,862,000

23. See *Handbook of Labor Statistical Work*, Statistical Publishing Company, 1958, Peking, p. 15; and Chung Wei-hsi, "My Opinion Towards the Classification of Personnel in Industrial Enterprises," *TCKT*, No. 11, 1957, p. 14.

24. This may not be true in some Western countries where workers' productivity and output are closely related to "depth" and quality of management.

25. See *JMJP*, editorial, July 17, 1955; *LT*, No. 8, 1955, pp. 3-4; *LT*, No. 18, 1958, pp. 19-20; *JMTY*, No. 6, 1958, pp. 26-27; and *CHKY*, No. 15, 1955, p. 6.

26. *Handbook of Labor Statistical Work*, p. 45; *TCK TTH*, No. 3, 1955, p. 41; Chang Hsu-hseng, *Approaches to Promote Labor Productivity in Our Socialist Industry*, Financial and Economic Publishing Co., 1956, Peking, p. 14; and Niu Chung-huang, *Accumulation and Consumption in the National Income of China*, China's Youth Publishing Company, 1957, Peking, pp. 101-2.

27. The enumeration of employment statistics was broadened in 1959. See Chen Chi-ho, "The Question of the Objective of Statistics in the Enumeration of Man Power," *CHYTC*, No. 11, 1959, pp. 27-30.

28. *Ibid.*, and SSB, *1956's Communique.*

29. *TCKTTH*, No. 2, 1954, p. 33.

30. See *JPRS*, 3234 (1960), p. 138. It must have meant 40 to 50 million man-days.

31. *JMJP*, Jan. 1, 1961.

32. Chen Chi-ho, *op. cit.*, p. 28.

33. A complete table is presented in the appendixes, showing the classifications of the industrial ministries in various years.

34. Yao Chuan, "Wage Plan," *CKKY*, No. 3, 1957, pp. 61-62.

35. Liu Ti-chen, "The Function and Aim of Wage Reform," *LT*, No. 5, 1956, p. 4.

36. That is, in terms of new Jen Min Pi which is equivalent to 10,000 yuan of old Jen Min Pi circulating before 1955.

37. For example, the prices of caustic soda produced by private enterprises and state enterprises were both quoted at 820 yuan per ton.

38. Methods of standardizing quantum units have been introduced and discussed by the Communist writers for certain commodities, such as converting tractors of different capacities into the standard set with 15 horsepower, trucks of different sizes into the standard size with 2 tons' load capacity, alcohol of different purities into 96° alcohol, cotton yarn of different count numbers

into standard count (21 counts) number, and all kinds of fuel into standard unit of 7,000 caloric. But in most cases it is not indicated whether this standardization procedure has been actually adopted in computing the quantity figures. See *TCKTTH*, No. 9, 1956, p. 29.

39. For the weights used here and other related information, see Table C-9 in Appendix C.

40. However, this treatment would inevitably introduce a downward bias to the production index of the steel industry for the years after 1952 and an upward bias for the years before 1952 because the proportion of quality steel to the total steel production would presumably be increasing as the steel industry developed. No solution can be found in regard to this problem. The weight, which is the representative price in this case, has to be fixed one way or the other.

41. For the official definition of metal cutting machines, see the footnote in *TCKT*, 1957, No. 18, p. 33. The average value of metal cutting machines in terms of tonnage is given as 10,000 yuan per 3.7 tons, or 2,703 yuan per ton. See Ching Lin "On the Proportional Relationship between the Metallurgy Industry and the Machine-Building Industry," *CHCC*, 1957, No. 9, pp. 11-15.

42. The exclusion of metal cutting machines would inflate the output index for the machine-building industry by 13.7 percentage points and the overall index by 1.2 percentage points in 1956.

43. Whether gas production is included in the gross value of industrial output as calculated by SSB is not known. There appear to be only two possibilities. First the value of gas production might be included in the gross output of those industrial enterprises of which gas is a by-product; or gas production might be counted, especially when gas is produced and distributed by independent companies, as part of the activities of the so-called "city services" departments of local governments. At any rate, our new indexes are to be understood as exclusive of gas production. Should the employment figures used in this study have included workers in the field of gas production, there would be some error. But this error must be very slight because gas production has never been a major industry in China.

44. Yu. N. Kapelinskiy, L. A. Kisvyantsev, M. S. Pankin, Yu. A. Nekshev, V. P. Senin and V. G. Sychev, *"Development of the*

Economy and Foreign Contacts of the People's Republic of China," 1959, Moscow. It is originally in Russian and translated by *JPRS*. The definition of aquatic production appears on p. 321, *JPRS* 3234 (1960). Also see the official definition given in *Brief Explanations on Terms of the First Five Year Plan*, People's Publishing Company, 1955, Peking, p. 31.

45. It was decided in 1958 that the defense industry should produce more than 50 types of civilian goods including IL-14 type planes for civil aviation, busses, 2.5-ton trucks, jeeps, shunting railroad engines, diesel locomotives, motorcycles, and bicycles. It was even proposed to have defense plants produce mining equipment, machinery for the chemical industry including large air compressors, 400 to 1000-ton hydraulic and oil presses, various machine tools, high frequency furnaces, and boring machines. The defense industry had also produced a large number of instruments and many types of household electrical appliances, radio sets, cameras, etc. See *JMJP*, November 12, 1958.

46. Statistical office of the United Nations, *Index Numbers of Industrial Production*, 1950, p. 10.

47. See *FFYP*, p. 57; *CHCC*, p. 16; Yu. N. Kapelinskiy and others, *op. cit.*, p. 195; and *CH*, p. 142. In the above cited writings the old classification is used. But in various issues of *China's Light Industry* (CKCKY) after 1957, they have used the new classification.

48. See *CKKY*, No. 11, 1953, p. 7; *CKCKY*, No. 16, 1955, p. 11; *HHKY*, No. 12, 1957, p. 3 and No. 18, 1959, pp. 1-9.

49. See *HHKY*, No. 1, 1958, p. 71; *JPRS* 6443, Dec. 1960, p. 9; *CCYC*, No. 2, 1959, pp. 34-36; and *FFYP*, p. 43.

50. See *HHPYK*, No. 6, 1957, p. 43 and No. 7, 1958, p. 51; *JMJP*, Feb. 20, 1957; *CH*, pp. 11 and 19, and *FFYP*, p. 42.

51. See the report of Hsueh Mu-chiao, former director of the State Statistical Bureau of the Central Government of Communist China, at the Fourth National Statistical Conference, as published in *TCKTTH*, 1955, No. 5, pp. 1-7.

52. Chia Chi-yun, "Conditions of the Statistical Work in 1954 and Opinions on the Statistical Work in 1955," *HHYP*, 1955, No. 4, p. 149.

53. State Statistical Bureau, "Instructions about the National Statistical Work in 1956," *HHPYK*, 1956, No. 8, p. 25.

54. Hsueh Mu-chiao's report at the Sixth National Statistical Conference, *TCKT*, 1957, No. 21, pp. 1-21.

55. See, for instance, *CHKY*, 1955, No. 1, p. 15 and *HHYP*, 1955, No. 2, p. 129.

56. For example, it is much easier and safer to embellish the gross value of production, which was another important "indicator" of the achievements of any enterprise. In fact, the statistical authorities in Communist China had learned from their own experience about the disadvantages of gross value of production and some other "indicators." Beginning in 1958, the twelve "mandatory indicators" that all industrial enterprises were previously required to report periodically were reduced to four, of which physical output is one.

57. There are three types of planned distribution of goods: (1) distribution by the central government, (2) distribution by various industrial ministries, and (3) distribution by local governments. About half of the producer goods output, in terms of 1955 gross value of production, is subject to the first type of distribution. See Li Keng-hsin, "Discussion on the Ways of Distributing Producer Goods in Our Country," *CHCC*, 1957, No. 8, pp. 18-22; and "Conference on the Distribution and Pricing of Industrial Goods," *CCYC*, 1959, No. 2, pp. 34-36.

58. For fuller discussions of the distribution system in Communist China, see Chi Kuang, "Inquiry on the Problems Concerning the Distribution Organizations of Producer Goods in Our Country," *CHCC*, 1958, No. 1, pp. 27-30, and Li Keng-hsin, *op. cit.*

59. Cases of returning defective merchandise to original producers are numerous and the returned goods are often in large amounts. For instance, the ratio of returned defective products to total sales of Shen-Yang High Pressure Switch Regulator Factory in 1955 was 50% (see *JMJP*, April 8, 1956); one-third of the locomotives sold by Dairen Locomotive Manufacturing Plant during the first quarter of 1956 were returned to the plant (see *JMJP*, Dec. 2, 1956).

60. *CHKY*, 1955, No. 1, pp. 8-10.

61. There are even one-man factories. See Yen Chun, "My Opinion on Several Statistical Problems Concerning the Newly Formed Industries," *TCYC*, 1958, No. 6, p. 39; and An Yu-shu and others, "Several Problems of Statistical Methods in the Industries Managed by Agricultural Cooperatives," *TCYC*, 1958, No. 8, pp. 26-30.

62. *Ibid.*

63. According to a sample survey made in April 1959, 70% of the products made by commune industries were consumed by the producing communes. See Ku Cho-hsin, "Development of Industrial Construction Planning in the Past Ten Years," *CHYTC*, 1959, No. 13, p. 15.

64. See Yen Chun, *op. cit.*, and *TCKT*, 1958, No. 23, p. 21. Another reason why some small industries have not kept production records is that they do not have measuring instruments such as large scales. See Chen Chi-ying, "Introducing a Method of Keeping Original Production Records for Indigenous Steel," *TCKT*, 1958, No. 3, p. 26, and Statistical Bureau of Szechuan Province, "On the Statistical Work for the 'Small Indigenous Group' of Steel and Iron Production," *CHYTC*, 1959, No. 1, p. 31.

65. Teng Chieh, *A Preliminary Evaluation of the Socialist Transformation of China's Handicraft Industries* (People's Publishing House, Peking, 1958) p. 101.

66. See, for example, Szu Tu-tsu, "Inquiry on the Methods of Calculating the Gross Value of Production of Local Industrials and the Gross Value of Agricultural Production," *TCYC*, 1958, No. 8, p. 31; Kao Yun-sheng, "Several Problems in Calculating the Gross Value of Production of Local Industries and the Gross Value of Agricultural Production," *TCYC*, 1958, No. 5, p. 24; and the previously cited articles by Li Keng-hsin and An Yu-shu. The dispute became more widespread in 1959 so that *CHYTC*, the official periodical of the State Statistical Bureau, devoted considerable space in the first few issues of 1959 to discussions on this topic under a special heading, "What Is the Reasonable Computation Method of Production Value for the Commune Industries?"

67. It may be offset, to some extent, by underreporting of enterprises. Cases of underreporting have been divulged, but not as frequently as cases of overreporting. They are usually the result of over-fulfillment of production plans. Some enterprises tend to hide part or all outputs that exceed the production quotas assigned to them for the current period for fear that their production quotas may be raised for the ensuing periods.

68. *JMJP*, Aug. 27, 1959.

69. Choh-ming Li, *The Statistical System of Communist China*, University of California Press, 1962, p. 149 and his "The First

Decade—Economic Development," *The China Quarterly,* No. 1, Jan.-March 1960, p. 35.

70. In calculating the utilization coefficient, all kinds of pig iron must be converted into the type of pig iron for making alkaline open-hearth steel or alkaline converter steel. The conversion rates for various types of pig iron have been determined and promulgated by the Metallurgical Industry Ministry. See *KYTCH,* pp. 367-68.

71. *KYTCH,* p. 379.

72. *KYTCH,* p. 379.

73. *KYTCH,* p. 356.

74. *CH,* p. 62.

75. *SLFT,* No. 5, 1958, p. 4.

76. *SLFT,* No. 4, 1958, p. 4.

77. See Table C-6 in Appendix C.

78. *KYTCH,* p. 367. Definitions pertaining to the utilization of blast furnaces are the following:

    Calendar days — time for major and medium repairs = statutory work-days

    Statutory work-days — time for cooling down = actual work-days

79. One Communist source indicates that due to the adoption of a new repair method in 1953, the actual time spent on "major repairs" of blast furnaces in that year was 30% shorter than the planned repair time. The output of pig iron resulting from the curtailed repair time was 23,000 tons (see *CH,* p. 24). This means that the actual time spent on "major repairs" in 1953 was about equivalent to the production time of $23,000 \times \frac{7}{3} = 53,667$ tons of pig iron. The national average utilization coefficient of blast furnaces in 1953 was given as 1.034 ton/m³ · day (*CH,* p. 25) and the interpolated annual average effective volume of blast furnaces in that year was 6,459 m³ (*CH,* p. 16). Therefore, the average time spent on major repairs of blast furnaces in 1953 should be

$$53,667 \div 1.034 \div 6459 = 8 \text{ days (24 hours each)}$$

    If we assume that the average time for major repair of blast furnaces is about the same for other years, then the average discrepancy in Test 4 can be cut down from 9.95% to 7.76%. It should be noted that this has not yet taken into account the time spent on "medium repairs."

80. The utilization coefficient of open-hearth furnaces is defined as

$$\frac{\text{Output of open-hearth steel}}{\text{Base area of open-hearth furnace} \times \text{calendar work-days}}$$

However, the way of counting work-days here is different from the case of blast furnaces. The relevant definitions are

Calendar days — time for major repairs = calendar work-days
Calendar work-days — cold-repair time = statutory work-days
Statutory work-days — hot-repair time = actual work-days
See *KYTCH*, p. 370.

81. See *TCKT*, No. 18, 1957, p. 33.

82. The definition is:

$$\text{coke ratio} = \frac{\text{total coke consumed } (1 - \text{degree of moisture})}{\text{total pig iron output}}$$

See *KYTCH*, p. 369.

83. The harvest period of cotton in China lasts from late August to the end of November, mostly in September and October. Raw cotton picked on the farm has to be dried and processed before it is brought to textile mills. See Feng Tze-fang, *China's Cotton*, the Financial and Economic Publishing Co., 1956, Peking, p. 106.

84. *CH*, p. 189, footnote (1).

85. *Brief Explanations of Terms Commonly Used in Industry*, Science Promotion Publishing Co., 1958, p. 78. It is said that most cotton cloth produced in Communist China is made of yarn of 22's. The actual distribution of yarns of various count numbers is given in *JPRS*, No. 756, 1958, as the following:

low count (below 20's)	10%
medium count (20's–26's)	70%
high count (above 28's)	20%

86. With the 20's yarn as 1, the standard conversion rate of 23's yarn is about 1.19. In other words, one bale of 23's yarn is equivalent to 1.19 bales of 20's yarn.

87. *TGY*, p. 108.

88. No standard deviation has been used here to determine the significance levels of sample means because the samples are not random ones. Besides, each of the national averages, if not invented by SSB, is a weighted average rather than an arithmetic mean of all plant figures in question.

89. The average heat values of coal consumed in thermal electric plants in the selected countries are given. See *OEEC, The Electricity Supply Industry in Europe*, Paris, 1956, p. 132. OEEC is the abbreviation used for the publication of the Organization for European Economic Cooperation.

90. See Watanabe Kisaku, *Fundamental Knowledge of Cotton Yarns and Cloth*, Tokyo, 1950, p. 23; and K. Saki, *The Cotton Industry in Japan*, Tokyo, 1956, p. 91.

91. Liu Yueh-shen and others, *Common Knowledge of Cotton Textile*, Textile Industry Publishing Company, 1955, Peking, p. 6.

92. *Brief Explanations of Terms Commonly Used in Industry*, 1958, pp. 77 and 79; and *Concise Dictionary of Scientific and Technical Terms*, Science and Technique Publishing Company, 1958, Shanghai, p. 703.

93. *KYTCH*, p. 379 and *TKP*, May 25, 1960.

94. *CH*, pp. 61, 62 and 74.

95. *CH*, p. 72.

96. See *OEEC, The Electricity Supply Industry in Europe*, 1956, Paris, p. 116.

97. *Ibid*. They are 90% and 86%, respectively, in 1953.

98. OEEC, "The Electricity Supply Industry in Europe," 1960, Paris, pp. 37-38.

99. *HCKTKY*, p. 90.

100. *Ibid.*, p. 91.

101. For the official definitions and related explanations regarding handicraft production, readers are referred to *HCKTKY*, pp. 87-99, and *Brief Explanations on Terms of the First Five Year Plan*, People's Publishing Company, 1955, Peking, p. 31; and *FFYP*, pp. 26-27.

102. See the footnotes attached to the tables of physical output figures in SSB, *1953-57's Communique* and *1958's Communique;* also see the footnotes on p. 166, *CH*.

103. The calculated gross value of handicraft output of the ten commodities in 1952 is 1288 million yuan which accounts for only 17.6% of the total gross output value of handicraft industry as officially given for 1952.

104. Ma Yen-chu, "The New Theory of Population," in *Documents of the Fourth Session of the First National People's Congress*, 1957, Peking, p. 314.

105. The gross value of factory production in 1952 is officially given as 27,020 million yuan (see Table 2).

106. *TCKT*, 1957, No. 18, p. 15.

NOTES TO CHAPTER V

1. That is: $8.8\% \times \frac{1}{2} \times .1576 + 5.0\% \times \frac{1}{2} .0204 = .74\%$ where .1576 and .0204 are the inter-industry weights for the metal processing industry and the chemical industry respectively.

2. To compute this percentage, we first add up the difference between the official gross value and the calculated gross value of included items, as of 1952, for each industry except the metal processing industry whose output value included military goods, and divide the resulting figure by the official gross value of total factory production in 1952. All figures needed are readily available in Table 15. The outcome is:
$$\frac{4,740}{27,020} = 17.5\%.$$

3. This category, of course, does not include the value of new goods produced after 1952.

4. Yu. N. Kapelinskiy and others, *op. cit.*, p. 84.

5. Many cases of private firms under-reporting production figures were disclosed during the "Five-Anti" movement in 1952.

6. For details of Liu-Yeh's computation, see T. C. Liu and K. C. Yeh, assisted by C. Twanmo, *The Economy of the Chinese Mainland: National Income and Economic Development, 1933-1959*, RM-3519-PR, the RAND Corporation, April 1963, Vol. I, pp. 78-96 and 219-41.

7. Here we are merely pointing out the fact. A separate study is needed to analyze in detail the factors contributing to the widely fluctuating path of economic development and its impact on the utilization of resources. It is interesting to note, however, that the Communist authorities have tried to rationalize the so-called "saddle-shaped" industrial growth by claiming it to be a normal pattern of development in a socialist economy. Se Liu Shiao-Chi "Report on the Government Works," *JMJP*, May 6, 1958. Other Communist economists attribute it to the fluctuation of agricultural crops. See *CHCC*, 1957, No. 7, pp. 4-8; Liu Jih-sin, "On the Relationship between Agriculture and Heavy Industry," *TKP*, Peking, Feb. 2, 1961; and Wang Ssu-hua, "The Role of Statistics in Our Economic Construction and Questions Pertaining to Some Statistical Indicators," *CCYC*, 1957, No. 5, p. 28.

8.   *HC,* Nos. 3 and 4, 1961, pp. 1-3.

9.   *JMJP,* Oct. 1, 1961.

10.   They are all base-weighted arithmetic means of quantities produced. Unless otherwise indicated, they include mining, manufacturing, electricity and gas. However, they vary in coverage and the weighting system used. The following table indicates the differences among the index series of the ten non-Communist nations to be compared.

	Scope and Coverage	Weighting System
Austria	Gas excl., covering 80% of the total net value of industrial production in 1937	Value added in 1937
France	Covering 83% of the total net value of industrial production in 1952	Value added in 1952
Western Germany	Covering 87% of the total net value of industrial production in 1950	Value added in 1950
India	Gas excl., covering 55% of the total net value of industrial production in 1951	Value added in 1951 as inter-industry weights, gross value of 1951 as intra-industry weights
Italy	Covering 84% of the total net value of industrial production in 1953	Gross value and value added in 1953
Japan	Covering 71% of the total net value of industrial production in 1955	Gross value and value added in 1955
Mexico	Gas excl., covering 90% of the net value of mining and 40% of manufacturing in 1944	Value added in 1944
Pakistan	Electricity & gas excl., covering 75% of the value added of mining & manufacturing in 1954	Value added in 1954
U.K.	Incl. construction, covering 85% of the total net value of industrial production in 1954	Value added in 1954
U.S.	Electricity and gas excl.	Value added in 1947

Sources: U.N. *Supplement to the Monthly Bulletin of Statistics,* 1959, pp. 29-44.

11. Norman M. Kaplan and Richard H. Moorsteen, *Indexes of Soviet Industrial Output*, RM-2495, the RAND Corporation, May 13, 1960; and G. J. Staller, "Czechoslovak Industrial Growth: 1948-1959," *American Economic Review*, Vol. LII, No. 3, June 1962, pp. 385-407.

NOTES TO APPENDIX A

1. For our discussions here, it may be appropriate to use two non-crossing production possibilities curves; but it is certainly not the general case. Two non-crossing production possibilities curves are assured only (1) when the economy in concern has grown rapidly and no resource has declined in quantity between the two periods, or (2) when, in the case of interspatial comparison, two countries are drastically different in size.

2. For detailed explanation of the graphical presentation of index numbers, see R. H. Moorsteen, "On Measuring Productive Potential and Relative Efficiency," *Quarterly Journal of Economics*, Vol. LXXV, No. 3, August 1961, pp. 451-455 and A. Bergson, *The Real National Income of Soviet Russia Since 1928*, Cambridge, 1961, pp. 31-34.

3. This situation may be depicted by the following graph in which OD/OA is greater than OE/OA.

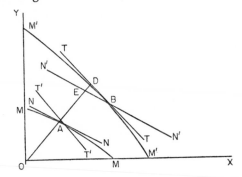

4. See p. 6.
5. A. Gerschenkron "The Soviet Indexes of Industrial Production," *Review of Economic Statistics*, Nov. 1947, p. 220, and his *A Dollar Index of Soviet Machinery Output, 1927-28 to 1937*, the RAND Corporation RM-197, April 6, 1951, pp. 46 and 52-54.
6. After production of a commodity is sufficiently expanded, there may also be some external economy in the form of reducing such business expenses as transportation costs and advertising costs per unit of product.

7. In most underdeveloped countries the average size of plants is smaller when compared with their counterparts in the highly industrialized countries. It is fairly safe to assume that the majority of industrial establishments in those countries have not reached the optimum sizes and that economy of scale may be achieved by enlarging the production units.

8. The intervals in U.S. dollars for each class are as follows:

Class I   200 and over
Class II   100–199
Class III   50–99
Class IV   Under 50

See U.N. Department of Economic and Social Affairs, *Patterns of Industrial Growth, 1938-1958*, New York, 1960, p. 437.

1. Chinese Publications and the List of Abbreviations

CB   *Current Background,* Hong Kong

CC   Yang Chien-pai, *Chung-Hua-Jen-Min-Kung-Ho-Kuo Hui-Fu Ho Fa-Chan Kuo-Min-Ching-Chi Ti Cheng-Chiu,* (Achievements in the Restoration and Development of the National Economy of the People's Republic of China), Statistical Publishing Co., 1956, Peking

CCCP   *Ching-Chi Chou-Pao* (Economic Weekly), Shanghai

CCTLKY   *Chien-Chu Tsai-Liao Kung-Yeh* (Building Materials Industry), Peking

CCYC   *Ching-Chi Yen-Chiu* (Economic Research), Peking

CFJP   *Chieh-Fang Jih-Pao* (Liberation Daily), Shanghai

CH   State Statistical Bureau, *Wo-Kuo Kang-Tieh, Tien-Li, Mei-Tan, Chi-Hsieh, Fang-Chih, Tsao-Chih Kung-Yeh Ti Chin-Hsi* (The Present and Past Conditions of Our Iron and Steel, Power, Coal, Machinery, Textiles, and Paper Manufacturing Industries), Statistical Publishing Co., 1958, Peking

CHCC   *Chi-Hua Ching-Chi* (Planned Economy), Peking

CHKY   *Chi-Hsieh Kung-Yeh* (Machinery Industry), Peking

CHYTC   *Chi-Hua Yu Tung-Chi* (Planning and Statistics), Peking

CKCKY   *Chung-Kuo Ching-Kung-Yeh* (China's Light Industry), Peking

CKFC   *Chung-Kuo Fang-Chih* (China's Textiles), Peking

CKKJ   *Chung-Kuo Kung-Jen* (China's Workers), Peking

CKKY   *Chung-Kuo Kung-Yeh* (China's Industry), Shanghai

CKLY   *Chung-Kuo Lin-Yeh* (China's Forestry), Peking

CN   *Chi-Nien-Lai Wo-Kuo Shih-Yin Kung-Shang-Yeh Ti Pien-Hua 1949-1956* (Changes in Private Industrial and

Commercial Enterprises in Our Country During the Last Seven Years) ed. by Chien Hua and others, Financial and Economic Publishing Co., 1957, Peking

FFYP *First Five-Year Plan for Development of the National Economy of the People's Republic of China in 1953-1957*, Foreign Languages Press, 1956, Peking

HC *Hung Chi* (Red Flag), Peking

HCKTKY Chao I-Wen, *Hsin-Chung-Kuo Ti Kung-Yeh* (New China's Industry), Statistical Publishing Co., 1957, Peking

HHKY *Hua-Hsueh Kung-Yeh* (Chemical Industry), Shanghai

HHPYK *Hsin-Hua Pan-Yueh-Kan* (New China Semi-Monthly), Peking

HHYP *Hsin-Hua Yueh-Pao* (New China Monthly), Peking

HP *Shang-Hai Chieh-Fang-Chien-Hou Wu-Chia-Tzu-Liao Hui-Pien 1921-1959* (Compendium of Data on Prices in Shanghai Before and After Liberation), Shanghai People's Publishing Co., 1958, Shanghai

JMJP *Jen-Min Jih-Pao* (People's Daily), Peking

JMTY *Jen-Min Tien-Yeh* (People's Power Industry), Peking

JPRS *U.S. Joint Publication Research Service Series*, Washington, D. C.

KJJP *Kung-Jen Jih-Pao* (Worker's Daily), Peking

KYCT *Kung-Yeh Chi-Tsai* (Industrial Equipment and Materials), Peking

KYTCH *Kung-Yeh Tung-Chi-Hsueh* (Industrial Statistics), Hupei People's Publishing Co., 1960, Hankou

LT *Lao-Tung* (Labor), Peking

MTKY *Mei-Tan Kung-Yeh* (Coal Industry), Peking

NCNA *New China News Agency*, News monitor

PH *Jen-Min Shou-Tse* (People's Handbook), Ta Kung Pao, Tientsin and Peking

SCMP *Survey of China Mainland Press*, Hong Kong

SJYHF Niu Chung-huang, *Wo-Kuo Kuo-Min-Shou-Ju Ti Chi-Lei Ho Hsiao-Fei* (The Accumulation and Consumption of National Income in China), China Youth Publishing Co., 1957, Peking

SLFT *Shui-Li Fa-Tien* (Hydroelectricity), Peking

SPKY *Shih-Pin Kung-Yeh* (Food Industry), Peking

SSB *State Statistical Bureau's Annual Communique on the Development of National Economy*, Peking

SSST   *Shih-Shih Shou-Tse* (Current Events), Peking
TCKT   *Tung-Chi Kung-Tso* (Statistical Work), Peking
TCKTTH *Tung-Chi Kung-Tso Tung-Hsun* (Statistical Bulletin), Peking
TCYC   *Tung-Chi Yen-Chiu* (Statistical Research), Peking
TGY   *Ten Great Years: Statistics of the Economic and Cultural Achievements of the People's Republic of China,* Foreign Languages Press, 1960, Peking
TKP   *Ta Kung Pao* (Impartial Daily), Tientsin and Peking
TTJP   *Tien-Ching Jih Pao* (Tientsin Daily), Tientsin
YCP   *Yeh-Chin Pao* (Metallurgical Bulletin), Peking

2. Non-Chinese Publications

BERGSON, A. *The Real National Income of Soviet Russia Since 1928.* Cambridge, 1961.

——. *Soviet Economic Growth.* Evanston, 1953.

CLARK, COLIN. *The Conditions of Economic Progress.* 2nd ed. London, 1951.

ECKSTEIN, A. *The National Income of Communist China.* New York, 1961.

FABRICANT, S. *The Output of Manufacturing Industries, 1890-1937,* NBER, New York, 1940.

FEDERAL RESERVE SYSTEM. "Revised Federal Reserve Monthly Index of Industrial Production," *Federal Reserve Bulletin,* Dec. 1953.

——. *Industrial Production, 1959 Revision,* Washington, D.C., 1960.

GEARY, R. C. "The Concept of the Net Volume of Output with Special Reference to Irish Data," *Journal of the Royal Statistical Society,* Vol. CVII, Parts III-IV, 1944.

GERMAN INSTITUTE FOR BUSINESS RESEARCH, *Weekly Report,* April 30, 1940.

GERSCHENKRON, A. "The Soviet Indices of Industrial Production," *Review of Economic Statistics,* Nov. 1947.

——. *A Dollar Index of Soviet Machinery Output, 1927-28 to 1937,* RM-1957, The RAND Corporation, April 6, 1951.

HICKS, J. R. "The Valuation of the Social Income," *Economica,* N.S. VII, May 1940.

HODGMAN, D. R. *Soviet Industrial Production, 1928-1951.* Cambridge, 1954.

HOLZMAN, F. D. *Soviet Taxation.* Cambridge, 1955.

KAPLAN, N. N. AND MOORSTEEN, R. H. *Indexes of Soviet Industrial Output,* RM-2595, The RAND Corporation, May 13, 1960.

KUZNETS, S. "On the Valuation of Social Income—Reflections on Professor Hicks' Article," *Economica,* N.S. XV, Feb. and May 1948.

LI, CHOH-MING. *Economic Development of Communist China,* Berkeley, 1959.

LITTLE, I. M. D. "The Valuation of Social Income," *Economica,* N.S. XVI, Feb. 1949.

LIU, TA-CHUNG AND YEH, KUNG-CHIA. *The Economy of the Chinese Mainland: National Income and Economic Development, 1933-1959,* Vol. 1 and 2, RM-3519-PR, The RAND Corporation, April 1963.

MILLS, F. C. *Statistical Method,* 3rd edition, New York, 1955.

MOORSTEEN, R. H. "On Measuring Productive Potential and Relative Efficiency," *Quarterly Journal of Economics,* LXXV, Aug. 1961.

NUTTER, C. WARREN. "Industrial Growth in the Soviet Union," *American Economic Review,* Papers and Proceedings, May 1958.

———. "On Measuring Economic Growth," *Journal of Political Economy,* LXV, Feb. 1957.

SAMUELSON, P. A. "Evaluation of Real National Income," *Oxford Economic Paper,* N.S. Vol. 2, Jan. 1950.

SETON, F. "The Tempo of Soviet Industrial Expansion," *Manchester Statistical Society,* Jan. 1957.

SHIMKIN, D. B. *Minerals—A Key to Soviet Power.* Cambridge, 1953.

STUVEL, G. "A New Index Number Formula," *Econometrica,* Vol. 25, No. 1, Jan. 1957.

UNITED NATIONS, STATISTICAL OFFICE. *Index Numbers of Industrial Production,* Studies in Methods, No. 1, New York, 1960.

———. DEPARTMENT OF ECONOMIC AND SOCIAL AFFAIRS. *Patterns of Industrial Growth, 1938-1958,* New York, 1960.

———. *Supplement to the Monthly Bulletin of Statistics,* 1959.

———. *Monthly Bulletin of Statistics,* July 1957 and Aug. 1960.

Index